THE LONDON HISTORY STUDIES

GENERAL EDITOR   R. BEN JONES

The Tudor Parliament

R. K. GILKES M.A.

 UNIVERSITY OF LONDON PRESS LTD

SBN 340 08072 8 Boards
SBN 340 08078 7 Paper

Sept 6'77
70-456947

University of London Press Ltd
St Paul's House, Warwick Lane, London EC4

Printed and bound in Great Britain by
Hazell Watson and Viney Ltd, Aylesbury, Bucks

EDITOR'S INTRODUCTION

THE LONDON HISTORY STUDIES are designed expressly for sixth-form students. They examine those events and personalities of the last five hundred years which continue to attract the attention of historians and arouse argument among them.

The books in the series are intended to be succinct and concentrated. Short quotations from contemporary sources are used both to enliven the text and to produce evidence to support particular arguments, while differing views of the principal historians are fairly represented. In addition to the facts, students should find a clear statement of the problems involved in each subject, presented in such a way as to ensure understanding and to stimulate thought. Short bibliographies give direction to further research.

The authors are practising sixth-form teachers who have been asked to write on the subjects in which they are especially interested. They are naturally familiar with the current research in their chosen fields but they can in addition draw on the knowledge and experience of the scholars and leading historians who compose the Advisory Panel. Thus the books contain the fruits of modern scholarship and are written from a close acquaintance with the questions that occur to students and the difficulties that face them.

It is hoped that this series will provide not only vigorous and effective treatment of the topics under discussion, but also an aid to a clear understanding of the methods of the historian.

R. B. J.

CONTENTS

PART I
Introduction

[1] THE GROWTH OF PARLIAMENTARY STATUS AND PRESTIGE UP TO 1629

The history of Parliament

There are four main stages in the history of Parliament. The first, which is the longest and the one we know least about, is the medieval period, extending from Saxon times to the middle years of the fifteenth century. The second and most formative stage lasts until 1688, and is the period which sees the House of Commons thrusting forward to become the dominant element in the Parliamentary trinity of King, Lord and Commons. From 1688 to 1832 is the aristocratic period; and the process of parliamentary reform initiated by the Great Reform Act of 1832 marks the beginning of the modern period of parliamentary development.

Importance of the period 1529–1629

It is the second of these periods which is the concern of this book, and, in particular, the years from 1529 to 1629, which are especially vital in the history of Parliament. In 1529 Henry VIII, frustrated in his Leviticus-based attempt to secure the annulment of his unfruitful marriage with Catherine of Aragon, yet still insisting upon a legal approach to the solution of his problem, issued writs for an assembly of Parliament.

In the space of its seven years' life this 'Reformation Parliament', as it was afterwards called, joined with the King to accomplish a revolution in the Church and in the State. The concerted attack on the authority of Rome, and the resultant aggrandisement of the monarchy was accomplished by a partnership between the King and the parliamentary classes, whose influence was strong in the City of London, the Law, in trade and commerce, and in the general administration of the country, both locally and nationally.

Never again was the Crown so powerful; its authority and high repute were lowered in the reigns of the bigoted Edward VI and the pitiful fanatic Mary, and, although Elizabeth restored the prestige of the Crown, she could not restore the impressive power her father had enjoyed. Moreover, the Crown–Parliament relationship, although it had stood firm for most of her reign, was, by the late 1580s, in sight of liquidation as the junior partner staked a claim for a greater share in the government of the realm, which the Crown was both unwilling and unable to grant.

The gauntlet, persistently, yet politely, waved over the whole course of Elizabeth's reign, was fiercely and frankly thrown down in the early decades of the seventeenth century. When Charles I dissolved Parliament in 1629, determined to 'go it alone', this very act acknowledged the reality of a new situation with the partnership already dissolved.

The seventeenth century and the antiquity of Parliament

The early part of the seventeenth century, which saw the achievement of parliamentary supremacy by a series of hardly contested victories, saw also the creation of the tradition of the antiquity of Parliament. Naturally enough the medieval historians and legal antiquarians were deeply interested in the genesis of Parliament, and men like Lord Chief Justice Coke in James I's reign pushed to the limits of credulity the extreme claim of Parliament to high antiquity.

The word 'parliament' itself gave ample scope for idealistic interpretation, and three etymologies were especially popular: *Parium lamentum* – 'where the peers lamented the grievances of the realm'; *Par-lamentum* – 'an equal and just complaint of all members of our nation, or sharing of grievances'; or, grandest of all, *Parlez-le-ment* – 'because everie member of that Courte should sincerely and discreetly speake his mind'. It was, however, a contemporary of Coke's – a man far less romantically inclined where Parliament was concerned – who destroyed the foundations of this tradition when he wrote:

When states are departed from their original Constitutions and that original, by tract of time worn out of memory, the succeeding Ages viewing the past by the present, conceive the former to have been like to that they live in, and framing thereupon erroneous propositions do likewise make thereon erroneous inferences and conclusions.

The medieval Parliament

The word 'parliament' means a 'conference', or 'parley', and was used to describe King John's meeting with his complaining barons at Runnymede, as it was even to describe the surreptitious meetings King Louis IX of France had with his wife on the palace backstairs just to get out of the way of his mother.

By 1250 the word was being actually used for conferences held by the King for the purposes of government. In Saxon times, the King, when he had a mind to, settled important matters with the counsel and consent of his thegns and leaders of the Church in the Witan.

Under the Norman kings this became a feudal court – the Great Council – and so it remained until the reign of Henry III, although the use of a jury by Henry II in 1188 to assess the Saladin Tithe had served to bring together the important ideas of taxation and representation.

In 1254 two knights, representing, not feudal tenants-in-chief, but the freemen of each county, were summoned to consider the financial help they were prepared to give to the King. In 1256, 1264 and 1265 they were called again, when Simon de Montfort, whose Victorian reputation was as 'Father of the

House of Commons', brought in also burgesses representing the
towns. His motive in doing this was to draw upon as broad a
basis of support for his plan of reform as he could, and the
desire for general support for certain ambitious projects was the
reason why Edward I carried on in the same way. He summoned two assemblies in 1283, one for the North, one for the
South, and to what has since been called the 'Model' Parliament
of 1295 he called the archbishops, bishops, abbots, barons,
lesser clergy, two knights from each shire, two citizens from
each city, and two burgesses from each borough – representatives,
that is, of the three classes into which medieval society could
be divided: those who prayed, those who fought, those who
worked.

In practice, the clergy (with the exception of the higher
clergy, who, after all, were not only landowners but feudal
lords as well) preferred to meet in their own assembly – Convocation; and, as the knights of the shires threw in their lot with the
citizens and burgesses, by the end of the fourteenth century
Parliament had become an assembly of two Houses – Lords
and Commons.

By the end of the fourteenth century, too, Parliament, which
was usually summoned when money was needed, had established
two very important principles of taxation: the King could not
impose direct taxes without its consent, while Parliament
could impose all kinds of taxes, direct and indirect.

In the fourteenth and fifteenth centuries Parliament's political
power grew considerably; Parliament resolved on Edward II's
deposition in 1327, and on Richard II's in 1399, and Edward IV
established good relations with Parliament by his bourgeois
tastes and general affability, where his pitiful predecessor, Henry
VI, and his turbulent Queen had created a mutual antipathy.

Indeed, Parliament was getting in some very good practice,
and its authority as a law-making assembly was already firmly
established; generally a Parliament had been a matter of but a
single session and, although Edward IV held only six Parliaments in the twenty-two years of his reign, the fourth had
the unprecedented number of seven sessions; this Parliament

lasted three years, and the total length of its sittings was ten months.

And there is another link with the later periods of parliamentary history: the enacting formula of Acts of Parliament – 'Be it enacted by the King's [Queen's] most Excellent Majesty, by and with the advice and consent of the Lords spiritual and Temporal, and the Commons, in this present Parliament assembled, and by the authority of the same, as follows . . .' – used since Henry VII's reign, had, in fact, grown into that form in this medieval period.

The 'Tudor Despotism'

The description of Tudor government as the 'Tudor Despotism' is generally looked upon now as a pious myth, fabricated by nineteenth-century historians, who made this claim from evidence drawn from too narrow a field. It seemed to them that the flood of directives sent out from London to the provinces, and bearing on all aspects of local administration, was ample testimony of an active and all-powerful government; but modern research, which has focused its attention on the provinces rather than on London, has shown that the complex provincial administration was really a most ramshackle affair, often corrupt and generally inefficient, so that even when the proclamations and other orders did get through from the capital there was no guarantee that they would be given a uniform and obedient implementation.

Moreover, it has also been shown that the Tudors did not attempt to become despotic rulers, for theirs was a monarchy limited by law, by Parliament and the Courts. However, this is not to say that the pendulum of academic interpretation has stopped swinging; for, when Professor Hurstfield poses again the question 'Was there a Tudor Despotism after all?' and answers that 'If the government of Henry VIII failed to establish, in the fullest sense, a Tudor despotism, it was not for want of trying', we can clearly anticipate some moderation of the already moderated traditional view.

Edward IV and Henry VII

The task in 1471, after royal authority had collapsed in the jumble of civil war, was to re-establish order and authority and rebuild the power of the Crown. In the next forty years, under Edward IV and Henry VII, efficient household government was indeed restored and the existing machinery of medieval government refurbished and re-employed; Parliament, which, by 1529, had met for just a few weeks in the course of thirty-two years, was in eclipse.

Henry VIII and Thomas Cromwell

The 1530s, however, saw the political scene transformed by the break with Rome, the establishment of a sovereign state, and the careful creation of the machinery of national government – all this the work, so Dr Elton has claimed (in *England under the Tudors*, Methuen, 1955), of Thomas Cromwell, 'the most remarkable revolutionary in English history', and this country's 'first parliamentary statesman'. Cromwell he sees as the man behind the Henrician reformation, a revolution in which Parliament was called to play its part, because both King and minister realized that only through Parliament could their revolution be legalized and enforced.

The legislation of the Reformation Parliament in the 1530s shows clearly Cromwell's belief in the supremacy of statute, just as it also acknowledges the supremacy of King, Lords and Commons as fully competent to deal with any matters – spiritual and temporal – that might arise. The result was surely a limited monarchy and not a despotism. Both partners gained from this alliance, built on the law as made by Parliament and implemented by the Courts; and the sovereignty of King-in-Parliament Henry himself made clear in 1543, when he told that assembly: 'We be informed by our judges that we at no time stand so highly in our estate royal as in the time of parliament, wherein we as head and you as members are conjoined and knit together in one body politic'.

In this joint enterprise the King, undoubtedly, was the senior partner. There is no conclusive evidence that either Henry VIII, or the other Tudors, 'packed' their Parliaments, but they did, in varying degrees, influence Parliament so that it was certainly not independent of the Crown; and Thomas Cromwell was a great manager of Parliaments.

Inside Parliament the main instruments of the King's guiding influence were the Speaker, who, although elected by the members of the House of Commons, was the nominee of the Crown, and the Privy Councillors, who, with the monarch, directed the course of Parliament, because they provided the parliamentary programme, which was carefully planned before each session. And Cromwell played an important part in this, as he did also in the careful 'softening up' of Parliament; if opposition was expected – and the Commons could be especially noisy when money grants were being asked for – then the views of individual members would be sounded, and the necessary conditioning and guidance would be imparted through preachers and official pamphleteers.

Here too the House of Lords was a source of strength, being almost solidly on the side of the King and assisting, on occasion, with the drawing up of Crown policy. More important, as much of the Council's legislation was put through the House of Lords first, then sent down to the House of Commons, the peers could, by their example, sway the opinion of the Lower House. Small wonder then that Cromwell could assure the King, as he did at the opening of the session in 1539, that there was 'never more tractable parliament'.

Considerable freedom of speech was permitted in Henry's Parliaments – even the mention of such a touchy subject as Catherine of Aragon was allowed to pass – but the generally short duration of the parliamentary sessions (and this also could be manipulated) inhibited excessive use of this liberty; there just was not the time for full-scale, searching debate – not that the government minded this, for after 1529 there was so much legislation to be introduced that neither King nor Council had any intention of lingering over it.

Here, of course, the Speaker's role was important; he could

cut short debate on one topic, almost exclude discussion of another, and a Privy Councillor's casual reference to the wishes of
the King was often enough to stifle opposition, as yet leaderless
and unorganized, from what was, after all, a loyal House of
Commons. Not that a numerical majority in the House was needed
to pass royal measures – the really vital need was for leaders and a
programme of legislation.

Nor must we forget the part played by Henry VIII in this.
If the acute political management of Cromwell could convoy the
royal policy to success it was undoubtedly speeded on its way by
the sheer personality of the King. In his prime his authority
and ruthlessness (and he was by far the most ruthless of the
Tudors) greatly impressed his Parliaments and his ministers.
At the end of his reign (and we have to look at the engraving by
Cornelius Matsys, published shortly after Henry's death, to feel
this) his aspect can have been little short of terrible; 'No man present at the sittings of Parliament dare for his life's sake open his
mouth or say a word, without watching the will of the King
and his Council', wrote Eustace Chapuys, the Imperial ambassador, to the Queen Dowager in 1547.

Edward VI and Mary

With the virtual collapse of royal authority after the death of
Henry VIII, the House of Commons was able to increase its
power considerably, but the period from 1547 to 1558 was too
short for the Commons to find leaders to organize their opposition – and there was much to complain about.

Somerset and Northumberland imitated Cromwell's methods
of management; for Somerset this may have contributed to his
downfall, but Northumberland would appear to have been more
subtle, and so, relatively, more successful. From 1549 to 1553
legislation proposed by the Council passed the Commons without
difficulty, probably because Northumberland's nominees for
parliamentary seats were the kind of members who would have
found their way into Parliament anyway, even without the aid
of the greater magnates or the country gentry.

In religion and government Mary favoured the medieval system, and here she ran into opposition from the House of Commons. Circumventing parliamentary disapproval of her disastrous marriage to Philip of Spain, she was, nevertheless, unable to move their refusal to allow her to drop either the name or the fact of the royal supremacy over the Church, or fulfil her desire for the full restitution of Church property. It has been suggested that Mary was up against a Protestant party in the House of Commons, but if such a group did exist it is surely significant that it did nothing to save the Marian martyrs.

Under Edward VI England came to the verge of civil war, while under Mary the very survival of the Tudor dynasty was at stake. Mary, the only Tudor with a conscience, yet the only one who really failed, exemplified the essential weakness of a woman ruler. She was, to John Knox at least, one of the three 'rotten props' (Mary, Queen of Scots and Catherine de Medici of France were the other two) against whom he directed his 'First Blast of the Trumpet against the Monstrous Regiment of Women'.

Elizabeth I

On the face of it, therefore, Elizabeth seemed to stand very little chance of success. It is a striking part of her great achievement as Queen that she turned the traditional weakness of her sex into a tower of strength – immune even from Knox's second trumpet blast. She restored the unity of England on foundations of peace and moderation, and by her quietly persuasive *via media* in both Church and State she was able to contain (certainly until the last decade of her reign) the problems that beset her, not the least of which was the growing ambition of the House of Commons.

The parliamentary classes – lawyers, merchants, country gentry – had steadily increased their influence since the thirteenth century. They it was who had benefited most from the break with Rome and the subsequent plunder of the wealth of the Church, as they were also the ones to gain from the inflation, which increased with the increase in the pressure of population (and, to some extent, with the influx of silver from the New

World) throughout the sixteenth century. One victim of this inflation, however, was the Queen herself, whose general revenue and income from land was, to a great extent, fixed. Now although the Crown did not become poor there was a relative decline in its authority, for what the Queen might, or might not do, was circumscribed by her weak financial situation.

Especially it meant that peace was essential (Henry VII was the only other Tudor to realize this); the cost of the day to day business of government and administration could barely be borne out of the Crown's income, but war, or indeed any commitment involving extraordinary expenditure, would send Elizabeth inevitably to Parliament for funds. It meant also that Elizabeth would have to rule within the existing structure of government, and this included Parliament.

In Elizabeth's reign the Privy Councillors still dominated Parliament, and it was now the Cecils who concerned themselves, as Thomas Cromwell had done, with details of legislation, with framing laws and speeches. Councillors served on every committee, and 'al the Privy Council of the House' would be included in a specially important one; and as the number of committees increased we find the influence of the Councillors even greater, because many M.P.s were not at all anxious to give up any more of their afternoons to committee work when they might be dealing with their own affairs, or those of their friends in the country.

The Speaker was still the spokesman of the Court, and the Council kept him strictly up to the mark; but the increasing use of committees (and larger ones at that) caused his power to wane as the reign progressed, for a Chairman of Committees was chosen entirely by the House.

Yet although the machinery of parliamentary management through the Council, and the Crown's control of patronage remained substantially the same, a strong Puritan minority, distressed by the Queen's Church Settlement and her failure to marry, was impelling the Commons to increase the rate at which they were moving towards what Professor Notestein has called 'the winning of the initiative'.

This indeed the Commons were doing by a greater organization and development of their parliamentary procedure, and, above all, by setting themselves to learn the art of successful opposition. By 1585 the difficulties of the Crown had grown: England was at war, and in the 1590s a series of bad harvests, associated with famine and plague and coupled with ever-rising prices, aroused widespread social discontent, which, in turn, merged into political discord.

Parliament, asked to grant money in taxes for war, took the opportunity to air their own complaints about the present discontents and proceeded to attack monopolies and other financial devices adopted by the Crown. Debates in the House were bitter and prolonged, preliminary rumblings of the stormy sessions of the 1620s. But this was not what was expected of the House of Commons, and Robert Cecil, the Queen's Secretary of State, was shocked to the core by such a parliamentary perform-ance in 1601, and declared their proceedings 'more fit for a gram-mar school than for a Parliament'.

Opposition to the Queen, however, was still small – the more vociferous firebrands, more often than not, were rusticated to the Tower – but contemporaries, 'very generally weary of an old woman's government', were painfully aware that the monarchy was in decline. The thoughts of the Commons in the 1590s were very much occupied with the future; respect for the Queen, her personal magic, still restrained them, but the situation, no doubt, would be very different under her successor.

James I

It was indeed, very different. 'Few kings', says Professor Note-stein of James I, 'have been so fitted by nature to call forth an Opposition and to put Government on the defensive.' Although James had long experience as a king in Scotland it had done him no good; in fact, in the English context it had done him positive harm. His views on the monarchy were substantially not very different from those of Elizabeth, but he must needs make them the text for continual sermons to his highly susceptible Parlia-ments. The subtle magic of the Tudor monarchy quickly evaporated; lesser men now surrounded the King, while those who were brilliant and worthy – Cecil, Cranfield, Bacon – never enjoyed his full confidence at all.

Now too, the leadership and organization, which the parliamentary opposition to the Tudors had lacked, strongly emerged at the expense of the Privy Councillors, whose power correspondingly declined. At the same time a great deal of solid work was done in committees and sub-committees, which whittled away the Speaker's influence still more, and even the House of Lords, for a time at least, moved over towards opposition.

One especially significant feature is the tremendous zeal and enthusiasm that the members of the Commons brought to their work at Westminster and, although Sir Thomas Smith's claim for Parliament that 'every Englishman is intended [i.e. is considered] to be there present' is very wide of the truth, members, nevertheless, were extremely sensitive to public opinion and deeply conscious of a need to report back to their constituencies; they had to show their constituents that they really had been working for the redress of grievances, and had not, as one member put it, 'bene all this while like children ketching butterflies'.

In the 1620s the parliamentary opposition to the Stuarts was out to catch much more than butterflies; it was seeking to gain for the House of Commons a measure of control over administration, as well as over legislation, and it was prepared to use the weapon of financial blackmail – the withholding of supply – as a means to that end. Charles I had no choice in 1629 but to dissolve Parliament and, had not 'the crass folly of his Scottish policy' (Plumb) led to war in 1639, which created the need for extraordinary expenditure and, therefore, Parliamentary aid (as Elizabeth had found after 1585), Parliament might quite well have remained for more than just eleven years in the wilderness.

Limited or absolute monarchy?

The argument put forward here is based upon the view that the form of government of Tudor England was a limited, or mixed monarchy, that is to say government based upon the consent of the governed. The question, however, is the subject of continuing debate among scholars.

Mr Christopher Hill maintains that 'the Tudor and early Stuart monarchy was an absolute monarchy of the continental type . . .'. The French historian, Roland Mousnier, holds this same view, and he defines an 'absolute monarchy' as one in which (although government actions did not require consent) the King was not allowed unlimited power, but his actions were measurable against certain accepted standards – custom, fundamental or natural law.

The mixed monarchy theory, however, derived from the political writers of antiquity, was the one accepted in the fifteenth and sixteenth centuries. Here was government by King, Lords and Commons, which represented in a balanced combination all the special attributes of monarchy, aristocracy and democracy. 'The things in dede', wrote John Aylmer in 1559, 'is to be sene in the parliament hous, wherin you shal find these 3 estats. The King or Quene, which representeth the Monarche. The noble men, which be the Aristocratie. And the Burgesses and Knights the Democratie.' Aylmer's contemporaries, the Jesuit, Robert Persons, the Puritan, Edmund Cartwright, and Sir Thomas Smith, the Elizabethan statesman, in their writings took the same view.

It was Sir John Fortescue, however, 'the most famous political theorist of the fifteenth century', who, says Professor B. Wilkinson,

made limited monarchy a characteristic feature of England, especially in contrast with France . . . He argues that the English king, unlike the French, might not make laws or impose taxes without the assent of the people. He did not argue that the people surrendered all share in government when they made their original constitution . . . King, Lords, and Commons, were all under the law of nature; but they were also all bound alike by the traditional laws of the land. The Common Law and the ancient customs formed England's bulwark against absolutism; the King received his powers to enable his subjects to enjoy their rights and property, not to oppress them . . . Finally, the English monarch had to rule with the agreement of his subjects in Parliament. They would not allow him to rule in any other way.

As we have seen, there was widespread acceptance of the mixed monarchy theory in the reign of Elizabeth and it had held the stage since the fifteenth century; but in the quarrels between James I and Charles I and their Parliaments, and during the eleven years of Charles's personal rule it appeared to have gone underground, and then, when the Civil War began, both sides recalled it and asserted that law-making properly belonged to the King, the Lords and the Commons.

It is the opinion of Miss C. C. Weston that this revival was due to Charles I's own adoption of the theory (as a tactical switch from Divine Right) in his Answer to the Nineteen Propositions of 1642, a document, which, she believes, 'contained one of the most influential declarations by an English monarch in modern English history'. In this Answer Charles spoke of

the ancient, equal, happy, well-poised, and never enough commended Constitution of the Government of this Kingdom', which 'the experience and wisdom of your Ancestors hath so moulded ... out of a mixture of these [i.e. absolute monarchy, aristocracy, democracy] as to give to this Kingdom (as far as human prudence can provide) the conveniences of all three, without the inconveniences of any one, as long as the balance hangs even between the three estates, and they run jointly on in their proper channel ...

He called the system a 'regulated monarchy', each of the estates – King, House of Lords and House of Commons – having powers of their own sufficient to check any misuse of authority by either of the other two. The 'proper channel' for the King's power was administration – matters of war and peace, 'making peers ... choosing officers and councillors of state, judges for law'; the role of the House of Commons, 'an excellent convener of liberty, but never intended for any share in government, or the choosing of them that govern', was to raise money and to impeach 'those who for their own ends ... have violated the law'. In the middle of the see-saw to keep the balance, sat the Lords, 'an excellent screen and bank between the prince and people, to assist each against any encroachments of the other [by their judicatory power], and by just judgments to preserve that law which ought to be the rule of every one of the three ...'

Both Royalist and Parliamentarian pamphleteers accepted this mixed monarchy theme, but growing disillusionment with the attitude and motives of the King in the negotiating period from 1646 to 1648 saw the spread of Leveller democracy within the Army and the end of the road for two of the three estates, if not, indeed, for all three.

Dr R. W. K. Hinton, on the other hand, argues that the early Tudor monarchy was a mixed one but its character changed, so that from the fifteenth century and Sir John Fortescue to the seventeenth century and Sir John Eliot the English monarchy had changed from a mixed to an absolute form; 'under Elizabeth, James I and Charles I', he claims, 'a single sovereign law-maker was in fact making law increasingly; and furthermore . . . was doing so with general approval'. This, Dr Hinton suggests, amounted to a 'decline of parliamentary government', because he finds that the 'output of unparliamentary government [documents issued in large quantities under the Great Seal, by the Signet Office and the Privy Council] follows an exactly opposite course to the output of Acts of Parliament. It rises under Elizabeth and the early Stuarts and falls off steadily (with a temporary rise under James II) from 1660 to the end of the century.' This growth of unparliamentary government, he believes, indicates the 'turning-of-the-back' on the idea of mixed monarchy.

He further claims that a decline in the 'idea of parliamentary government' is apparent from the expressed opinions of the Crown lawyer, Sir John Davies, Sir Edward Coke, 'who stood for the sovereignty of the law, not for the sovereignty of Parliament', and Sir John Eliot, who declared that supreme power lay with the King alone, for 'he was to make any law which was for the good of the commonwealth'. The effect of such views, Dr Hinton concludes, was to elevate the status of the King at the expense of the status of Parliament, and to allow the King to be regarded as absolute.

Mr J. P. Cooper does not accept Dr Hinton's idea of a decline of parliamentary government, on the grounds that contemporaries would not have looked upon letters patent and Acts of Parliament as the same thing at all; letters patent could be challenged in the courts, could be revoked by the King alone, but a statute could only be revoked by the King-in-Parliament.

Nor is the output of Acts of Parliament necessarily a reliable guide to parliamentary activity. Surely, it was in just these periods when the output fell that the members of the House of Commons were most vociferous in expressing their concern at the attitudes and policies of the Crown, and at such times – irrespective of the number of bills passed – the influence of Parliament can hardly be thought of as in decline.

As for Dr Hinton's claim that general approval had been given to the King as sovereign law-maker, Mr Cooper points out that the Commons in their Apology of 1604 denied that the King 'had any absolute power . . . either to alter religion . . . or to make laws concerning the same, otherwise than as in temporal causes by consent of Parliament . . .'. Similarly, the Commons' Petition of 1610 made clear that 'the policy and constitution of this your kingdom appropriates unto the kings of this realm with the assent of Parliament, as well the sovereign power of making laws as that of taxing . . . Out of this root hath grown the indubitable right of the people of this kingdom not to be made subject to any punishment that shall extend to their lives, lands, bodies and goods, other than such as are ordained by the common laws of this land or the statutes made by their common consent in Parliament.'

In 1610, 1614 and 1621 the Commons attacked proclamations and the idea that they could, in fact, make law, while James I himself disdained to claim any such power 'by his proclamations wch might seem to challenge to them selfs the nature of laws wch [was] a power certenly only in the parlement to inacte'.

As for the claim that England's was an absolute monarchy on the continental pattern, Mr Cooper allows that although Bodin's ideas were widely known in England their impact was relatively slight, perhaps because Englishmen could look abroad and see for themselves how ideas of absolutism worked out in practice; 'there were', he concedes, 'at least the possibilities of similar developments under the early Stuarts; even in the parliamentary sphere, if the attempts of Salisbury and Cranfield to solve the Crown's problems had been successful, the similarities with other assemblies might have been greater. But in fact the Civil War, though in some ways a reflection of forces generally at work in Europe, finally consolidated a pattern very different from that of most European states.'

It may well be, as so often is the case, that the truth lies somewhere in between, or, indeed, across these rival views. Certainly the definitions of limited and absolute monarchy are not very helpful. In many ways – in his decision to make war or peace, or to dissolve Parliament, for example – the monarch was indeed absolute in that his action did not require the consent of the people; but in many ways too, and in taxation above all, his will was limited by the assent of his people, expressed through Parliament; while the law-making process itself, dependent as it was and is upon the collective agreement of King, Lords and Commons, imposed an obvious limitation on both the action and the will of the sovereign.

Further Reading

*J. W. ALLEN, *A History of Political Thought in the Sixteenth Century*. Methuen University Paperbacks (London, 1960).

*J. P. COOPER, 'Differences between English and Continental Governments in the Early Seventeenth Century', in *Britain and the Netherlands*, edited by J. S. Bromley and E. H. Kossman. Chatto and Windus (London, 1960).

R. H. EVANS, *Government*. Studio Vista (London, 1964).

*J. W. GOUGH, *Fundamental Law in English Constitutional History*. Oxford University Press (London, 1961).

*R. W. K. HINTON, 'English Constitutional Theories from Sir John Fortescue to Sir John Eliot', *English Historical Review*, Vol. LXXV (July 1960).

*R. W. K. HINTON, 'The Decline of Parliamentary Government under Elizabeth I and the Early Stuarts', *Cambridge Historical Journal*, Vol. XIII (1957).

*HAROLD HULME, 'Charles I and the Constitution', in *Conflict in Stuart England: Essays in Honour of Wallace Notestein*, edited by William Appleton Aiken and Basil Duke Henning. Jonathan Cape (London, 1960).

D. L. KEIR, *The Constitutional History of Modern Britain 1485–1937*. Black, 6th ed. (London, 1961).

EDWARD MILLER, *The Origins of Parliament*. Historical Association
    Pamphlet, General Series, No. 44 (London, 1960).
CHRISTOPHER MORRIS, *Political Thought in England from Tyndale to
    Hooker*. Oxford University Press 'Home University Library'
    (London, 1953).
A. R. MYERS, 'Parliaments in Europe: The Representative Tradition'
    Part I: *History Today*, Vol. V, No. 6 (June 1955).
    Part II: *History Today*, Vol. V, No. 7 (July 1955).
WALLACE NOTESTEIN, *The Winning of the Initiative by the House of
    Commons*. British Academy (London, 1924).
*C. C. WESTON, 'The Theory of Mixed Monarchy under Charles I and
    After', *English Historical Review*, Vol. LXXV (July 1960).
*B. WILKINSON, *Constitutional History of England in the Fifteenth
    Century, 1399–1485*. Longmans (London, 1964).

    * These books and articles form the basis of the argument on 'Limited or
Absolute Monarchy' given in this chapter.

PART II
The Mechanics of Parliament

[2] COMPOSITION

The Tudor Parliament can only be understood within the Tudor context; it cannot be judged by nineteenth and twentieth-century notions of what Parliament is and should be. What to us appears scandalous – patronage, rotten and pocket boroughs, the whole gamut of political hanky-panky that would cause a good democrat to throw up his hands in disgust and despair – troubled our sixteenth-century ancestors not at all; for these things were simply part and parcel of their own political way of life.

Living under an established parliamentary democracy we must remember that the sixteenth century was the period of parliamentary apprenticeship, when the Tudor rulers, by employing a cooperative assembly to achieve their policies, thereby fashioned an institution strong enough to reduce their own powers.

Yet the centre of government in this period was still the Royal Council. Parliament was an extraordinary, not an ordinary part of the constitution, and its use as an instrument of royal action was still only occasional. It met when summoned to do so by the King; it was dissolved at his own pleasure, and it was certainly not part of its business to exercise supervision over the government of the country.

Frequency and duration of Parliament

Medieval Parliaments seldom had more than one session, and 'continuous parliamentary government was neither expected

nor desired'; attendance was irksome for the knights and burgesses, and their constituencies, which paid them wages (at the
rate of four shillings a day for county members, two shillings a
day for borough members) and travelling expenses, were understandably well content with few Parliaments and short sessions.

After the Wars of the Roses Parliaments were summoned less
frequently than they had been in the Yorkist period; there
was, after 1485, no aristocratic opposition left to demand them,
and the new King made very few demands for taxation as he
could manage very well with his ordinary revenue from the Crown
lands – now much augmented by post-rebellion confiscations –
customs, feudal dues and what became for him the lucrative
profits of justice.

Henry VIII summoned nine Parliaments, but the 'Reformation
Parliament' of 1529–36 was of unprecedented length, although
its sessions were still short; it met in seven sessions (as indeed
had Edward IV's last Parliament) but the cumulative length
of its sessions amounted to nearly eighteen months, as against
the ten months of Edward IV's. 'Roughly speaking, the Reformation Parliament sat longer than all the Parliaments of Edward IV
or all those of Henry VII put together, and thirty per cent.
longer than Henry VIII's own Parliaments during the first twenty
years of his reign' (Pollard), and we must remember that from
22 December 1515 to 15 April 1523 there was no Parliament
at all.

The first of Edward VI's two Parliaments, from 4 November
1547 to 15 April 1552, met in five sessions, the longest being less
than three months, and of Mary Tudor's five Parliaments, while
the shortest lasted for something less than a month, the longest
was still less than two.

The total parliamentary time in Elizabeth's reign amounted
to 140 weeks – ten Parliaments, with sometimes three, four, or
nearly five years between them, but only thirteen brief sessions
in a reign of almost forty-five years. The length of these sessions
ranged between four weeks and two days in 1576 to fourteen
weeks and six days in 1559, with an average duration of under
ten weeks; indeed, the evidence shows that the Queen kept

Parliament to a pretty tight working schedule, through the
Speaker in the Commons and through Burghley in both the Commons and the House of Lords.

Elizabeth's second Parliament, summoned on 12 January
1563 and dissolved on 2 January 1567, met in only two sessions,
the first from 12 January 1563 to 10 April 1563, the second
from 30 September 1566 to 2 January 1567; while her fourth
Parliament, whose life was from 8 May 1572 to 19 April 1583,
held only three sessions in 1572, 1576 and 1581.

The picture is still very much the same in the early Stuart
period, when parliamentary sessions covered no more than four
and a half years of the period from the accession of James I in
1603 to the assembling of the Long Parliament in 1640. Of course
the eleven years between 1629 and 1640 when Charles I managed
without Parliament was an unprecedented interval, but his
father had called no Parliament after the dissolution of his first
in 1610 until April 1614, nor from June 1614 to January 1621, nor
between December 1621 and February 1624, and Charles himself was responsible for the long prorogations which are a feature
of the parliamentary history of his reign.

It follows, therefore, that Parliament was an amateurish body,
very much at a disadvantage (certainly until the end of the sixteenth century) in knowledge and experience of parliamentary
affairs and political techniques vis-à-vis the royal servants, the
Privy Council, who, working with the Crown, could carry on the
government of the country when Parliament was not in session.

Infrequent Parliaments also militated against the growth
within Parliament of an organized opposition to the Crown, for
the many new members who assembled when Parliament met
needed time to get to know one another, and here, of course,
the short sessions did not help.

By 1386 it could be asserted that 'the law of the land is made
in parliament by the king and the lords spiritual and temporal
and all the commonalty of the realm'. The names 'House of
Lords' and 'House of Commons' came into use in the sixteenth
century, although they were actually there in the fifteenth
century as the 'Higher House' and the 'Common House'. In the

Tudor period when we speak of Parliament it is really the House
of Commons that we have in mind, but some mention must be
made here of the House of Lords, which was, after all, an essential
part of the machinery for the government of the country.

The House of Lords

The House of Lords under the Tudors was, on the whole, a com-
plaisant body and presented no problem. Both lay lords – Peers
of the Realm – and spiritual Lords – Lords of Parliament – were
closely bound to the Crown. Before the Wars of the Roses the
lay peers were feudal magnates holding great estates and exercising great military and local power, while their spiritual
counterparts were great independent prelates, or the representatives of wealthy and powerful corporations; after the period of
civil war the situation had changed, for the lay lords found that
status now depended on their holding an important office of
state under the Crown, and the spiritual lords, who had been in
the majority in the Higher House in Henry VII's reign, and from
whose ranks the King had chosen his officials and confidants,
after the establishment of the Royal Supremacy found themselves
merely nominees and employees of the Crown.

In the fifteenth century the number of temporal peers summoned to Parliament had rarely been more than 50 (53 had attended the Parliament of 1454, the last before civil war broke
out) but the Wars of the Roses had knocked the stuffing out of
the lay peerage and only 29 received writs of summons to the
first Parliament of Henry VII's reign. Of these only 18 attended,
and this was not because the old families had been wiped out in
the wars, but because some were excluded who had been attainted,
a few from the North were not summoned, and others were
minors who took their seats later.

The Tudors did not often create new peerages. Henry VII
added only five, Henry VIII thirty-seven, seventeen of them in
the last eight years of his reign; but two of his four dukes
he executed. Elizabeth simply filled up the gaps created by peerages becoming extinct, and it is significant that the new names

among her creations – Cecil, Dudley, Russell, Sidney, Sackville,
Wentworth, Wriothesley, Paget, Howard, Cavendish, Herbert
are all English, as distinct from the names of the old feudal
baronage; at the end of her reign there were still only fifty-
nine temporal peers.

With the accession of James I, however, the composition of
the House of Lords was considerably modified. On 4 May 1605,
he created or promoted eight peers, and by 1610 their numbers
had been increased to eighty. Buckingham's policy of the large-
scale sale of peerages – baronies at £10,000 each, viscountcies
at £15,000, earldoms at £20,000 – brought the numbers in the
House to 126 by 1628, but the result was not what had been
intended. The older peers were greatly offended, the new peers'
loyalty could not be relied upon; and in 1621, 1626 and 1628 the
Lords allied with the Commons to inflict heavy defeats on
James and his son.

The most significant change in the composition of the House
of Lords, a change carried out with parliamentary sanction, was
undoubtedly the reduction in the number of the spiritual peers
as the result of the dissolution of the monasteries in 1536–40.
The archbishops, nineteen bishops, twenty-eight mitred abbots
were summoned to his Parliaments by Henry VII, and his son
added three mitred abbots to the number of spiritual peers.
But at the dissolution all thirty disappeared, and the proportion
of lay to spiritual peers was completely reversed; instead of 49
spiritual peers meeting with 29 lay lords, after the dissolution
there were only 26 bishops and between 36 and 50 lay members of
the Upper House.

The presence of the occupants of the six bishoprics created by
Henry VIII out of the monastic spoils (one of which – Westminster – ceased to exist when its first bishop was translated to
another see in Edward VI's reign) went only a short way towards
redressing the balance. From this time, in fact, and as new lay
peerages were created, the influence of the spiritual lords waned,
and as the break with Rome gave the Crown complete control
over the composition of the episcopate the ecclesiastical element
in the House of Lords could be relied upon for its support.

It would seem that the lay peerage was less subject to Crown control. Under Henry VII and Henry VIII Chancery writs of summons were issued with almost complete regularity, which suggests that the Crown no longer had the power to withhold them, although under Henry VII the King was not obliged to accept the rule that a baron, once summoned, would always be summoned and his heirs after him. Nevertheless, the Crown's hold over the House of Lords was sufficiently strong and little management was necessary. Indeed the Crown might advise some lords to stay away if their presence was not regarded as desirable, and then there was attached to the writ of summons under the Great Seal an intimation, under the Privy Seal, that the writ was not to be obeyed; on the other hand fines could be imposed in cases of undesired non-attendance. But in the Tudor period there had emerged a new nobility to replace the ancient families rivalling the Crown, whose community of interest with the Crown made them loyal and useful supporters of royal policy. Only one dukedom – that of Norfolk – existed after 1554, and after the execution of the fourth Duke, 'the last aristocratic champion of reaction' (J. B. Black), for his complicity in the Ridolfi Plot, the title was not revived for fifty years, and no new dukedom was created until Buckingham's in 1623.

One further change in the composition of the House of Lords was the result of the emergence among the temporal lords of the principle of a hereditary right of summons, which led to the creation of a defined lay peerage. This led to the exclusion from the Upper House of the royal officers – judges, Attorney-General, Solicitor-General, the King's Serjeants, and, most important of all, the Chancellor – who had received writs of summons and sat like lords in their capacities as servants of the Crown. A statute of 1539 declared that those royal officers below the rank of baron, yet sitting as members of the House of Lords, could have 'not interest to give any assent or dissent' in the proceedings of that House, and so they were to become mere assistants with no power to vote.

Sometimes the Chancellor was made a peer to become a full member of the House of Lords, although this was not regular procedure until 1705; but the others – judges, law officers, Privy Councillors too, turned their attention to the Lower House, secured seats, and sat 'as elected representatives instead of as crown nominees' (A. F. Pollard in *The Evolution of Parliament*, Longmans, 2nd ed. 1926). That Privy Councillors preferred to seek election as members of the House of Commons is surely significant in that it provides further clear evidence of the growing importance of that House in the Tudor period, while the entry of the Privy Councillors undoubtedly increased its prestige. It is to the Lower House and its composition that we must now turn.

Membership of the House of Commons

The most striking feature of the House of Commons in the sixteenth century, and again indicative of its growing importance, is the great increase in its membership. An assembly of 296 members at the beginning of the century, in the latter part of Elizabeth's reign had become an assembly of 462, an increase of more than a half. From the accession of James I to the first Parliamentary Reform Act of 1832 a further 51 English seats were added, no less than 45 of them being additions from the reigns of James I and Charles I, so the Tudor expansion phenomenon persisted into the early Stuart period.

At the beginning of the sixteenth century all the English counties, with the exception of Durham, elected 2 Members of Parliament, in all 74 county members; the remaining members sat as representatives of a large number of parliamentary boroughs. Now there was no particular reason, other than custom, why one borough should be represented in the House of Commons when others were not, and the Tudor sovereigns, Elizabeth above all, continued the creation or revival of parliamentary boroughs which had been begun by royal charter in 1445.

Borough creations

Even as early as this the pressure was building up for parliamentary seats; already the appeal of membership of the House of

Commons had fired the ambition of the ubiquitous country gentle-men. These borough creations, from the fifteenth century on-wards, conformed to no logical pattern of priority. For example, Henry VI enfranchised several sizeable and important boroughs – Plymouth, Coventry, Poole and Chippenham; but others, like Bramber, Steyning and Gatton, were very small and insignifi-cant. Taken together Bramber and Steyning, only half a mile apart, were no larger than a single village, yet they were given two seats each, while Gatton had become deserted a century later but survived as a notorious rotten borough until 1832.

Henry VIII added 38 new members of Parliament to bring the total membership to 334, by granting two representatives to each of the boroughs of Berwick-on-Tweed, Buckingham, Lancaster, Newport (in Cornwall), Preston, Orford and Thetford; and, in 1543, four representatives for the County Palatine of Chester – two for the County, two for the city of Chester itself.

The port of Calais sent burgesses to the House of Commons from 1536 to 1555, and in 1536 Wales was included in the repre-sentative system. By an Act of that year one knight was to be returned for each of the twelve Welsh counties, two for the county of Monmouth, and one burgess for each county town except Merioneth, and two for the borough of Monmouth. The Act prescribed for 'the election to be in like manner, form and order, as knights and burgesses of the Parliament be elected and chosen in other shires of this realm', that is to say it established the forty-shilling freeholder franchise. It further provided for the payment of Welsh members after the manner of their English counter-parts, even though by 1536 wages were not generally being paid by English constituencies, and, in fact, wages were probably never, as a general rule, claimed by the members for the Welsh counties and boroughs.

One clause of the 1536 Act had made towns other than the shire towns then enfranchised liable for contributions to the wages of the representatives of those shire towns; and, although the right to elect was only specifically granted to the shire towns, the implication was that these contributory towns would, at the same time, be entitled to take part in the election of those representatives. This did not, in fact, happen, and it was in response to popular demand for a definite extension of this right to elect to the contributory towns that a second Act for Wales was passed in 1543, declaring that the contributory towns 'shall have like voice and authority to elect and choose the burgess of every said shire town, like and in such manner as the burgesses of the said shire towns have or use'. The shire towns, however, wanted to elect their burgesses free from the participation of their contributory towns, and in Edward VI's reign Beaumaris successfully shook off its electoral connection with Newborough, its only contributory borough, and became the first Welsh borough to be really self-contained for parliamentary purposes; a new charter, granted by Elizabeth in 1562, vested the right to elect the member for Beaumaris in the municipal corporation.

The royal Duchy of Cornwall enjoyed political notoriety in 1832 as being grossly over-represented in the House of Commons and swarming with rotten boroughs. Before the Tudor period, however, the duchy had not been over-represented, indeed only six boroughs had continuously sent members to Parliament; but Edward VI, whose 17 enfranchised boroughs added 34 members to the House of Commons, anticipated this reputation when he included in the creations made in his second Parliament of 1553 seven Cornish boroughs – Bossiney, Camelford, St Michael, Penryn, Saltash, West Looe, and Grampound, later to be described as 'a synonym of electoral squalor and corruption' (E. & A. G. Porritt), and disfranchised in 1821.

Mary Tudor disfranchised one borough – Maidstone – as punishment for the part it had played in the rebellion of Sir Thomas Wyatt, but she also added 14 more. Aldborough (Yorkshire), Aylesbury, Boroughbridge, Castle Rising, Droitwich, Knaresborough, Morpeth, Ripon, St Albans, St Ives, and Woodstock returned two members each, but, somewhat unusually, three – Abingdon, Higham Ferrers, and Banbury – were single-member constituencies, the latter being granted its charter and parliamentary privilege out of gratitude for its support in the troubled period of the Queen's accession.

390 members sat in the House of Commons in Elizabeth's first Parliament, which met on 25 January 1559 and, had all constituencies made returns and been represented, the number would have been 400; by the end of her reign 62 seats had been added.

Of all the Tudors Elizabeth was the most prolific restorer and creator of parliamentary boroughs, although it must be remembered that hers was also the longest reign. A minority of these boroughs was created by clauses in letters patent of incorporation granted at the request of the locality itself with the support of its lord and patron. 'Two burgesses were admitted into the High Court of Parliament', for example, for the borough of Newport, Isle of Wight, enfranchised along with nine others in 1594, 'at the special instance of Sir George Carey', but most were either boroughs which had allowed their right to send representatives to lapse and now had it restored, or boroughs which were enfranchised by a precept from the Sheriff, who cannot have acted entirely of his own volition, but must have received a special writ from the Chancery, which in turn must have received a warrant from the Crown.

Now certainly many of these boroughs were rotten boroughs from the beginning to the end of their story, but they were not created, as used to be thought, so that the Queen could pack Parliament; the researches of Sir John Neale have shown that, whether the boroughs were enfranchised by charter, by restoration of parliamentary right, or by sheriff's precept derived from the Crown, always the initiative came from the boroughs themselves, reacting to the pressure being put on them by the country gentry.

Had these new parliamentary boroughs consistently returned royal nominees or out-and-out government supporters the case would be very much altered, but they did not; Cornwall, for example, had Elizabeth intended it, might have been a nursery of royal officials; but men like Paul Wentworth, M.P. for Liskeard 1572–87, and his elder brother, Peter, who sat for Tregony 1576–83, were members of great courage and conviction, whose undoubted independence of mind made them immune to sycophancy.

The desire to sit in Parliament, the keen and oftentimes unscrupulous rivalry between prospective candidates, did not arise from political differences but from local family and personal rivalries for local prestige and glory. Although Elizabeth yielded to this pressure to create parliamentary seats in 1559, 1563, 1571, 1572, 1584 and 1586, local demand was not always accepted by the Crown. The Earl of Rutland's plea for the enfranchisement of Newark in 1579 was rejected, perhaps because Elizabeth herself believed the process had gone far enough, on the grounds 'that there are over many burgesses already'. Her resolution weakened, however, only five years later when she agreed to ten borough creations; but, except for the final enfranchisement of her favourite Leicester's borough of Andover in 1586, she had gone as far as she intended to go. When she had spoken, in her reply to the Earl of Rutland, of 'a device hereafter to lessen the number of divers decayed towns' she had demonstrated her awareness of the need for some measure of parliamentary reform, but that some 'device' to achieve it could be introduced was not really likely as the situation had been created by forces in the country which the Crown had been unable to restrain.

Borough enfranchisement continued under James I and Charles I. James granted charters of enfranchisement to Bury St Edmunds, Tewkesbury, Tiverton, Bewdley, Evesham and Harwich – all towns of some importance, and the right to return members to Parliament was revived for Ilchester, Hertford, Wendover, Amersham, Marlow and Pontefract. Of the 27 members added to the House of Commons 4 sat after 1603 as representatives of the universities of Oxford and Cambridge.

Since 1570 six petitions for their enfranchisement had been presented by the two universities; their contention was that as Acts of Parliament had been passed concerning the universities it was both reasonable and necessary that they should have their own burgesses to keep Parliament accurately informed on the state of the universities, and also to safeguard university interests should any further legislation concerning them be contemplated. The chief patrons of the universities' claim were the Chancellor of the University of Cambridge, Lord Burghley, and the redoubtable Attorney-General, Sir Edward Coke. Coke in 1593 had spoken of the desirability of enfranchising Oxford and Cambridge, and, not surprisingly, had advised them to choose civil lawyers as their representatives; his advice was taken, and in choosing, as their charters put it, 'two of the more discreet and sufficient men of the university for the time being', both universities returned doctors of civil law to the Parliament of 1604. In the reigns of both James I and Charles I strong Court influence was exerted upon the universities, and royal direction was particularly strong in the choice of Cambridge M.P.s. Oxford's loyalty to the Crown was to be tested and tried by the second of the Stuarts and tried beyond endurance by his Catholic son.

Attendance in the House of Commons

After what has been said about the great increase in the number of members of the House of Commons and the mounting pressure from the country gentry for seats in Parliament, it is pertinent at this point to consider the general level of attendance among M.P.s. The picture is an interesting one. Although 'knights and burgesses regarded attendance at parliament as a matter of very great importance at the end of the fourteenth century and valued their right to be present and to represent the communities of the shire and borough' (B. Wilkinson in *The Constitutional History of Medieval England*, Longmans, 1952), the communities themselves would not appear to have been so minded, for we find that M.P.s who stayed the shortest time in the House 'afforded the greatest amount of satisfaction to themselves and their fellow townsmen' (E. & A. G. Porritt); even in 1532, when ambitious men looked to Parliament, Canterbury gave John Bridges, one of its members, a sum of money 'towards a bonet for saving the wage that he should have had of the city by reason of his being at home from the Parliament after Easter term'.

Absenteeism was, in fact, a real problem in the whole Tudor period, as there existed no machinery to compel an M.P. to be in his place promptly on the opening day and to attend each morning, six mornings a week, during the session. Regular attendance for just a short session was a wearisome business, and just how jaded an M.P. could feel was summed up by Thomas Cromwell in a letter written in 1523 when he had re-entered Parliament and had sat through a long session:

I, amongst other, have indured a parliament, which continued by the space of seventeen whole weeks, where we communed of war, peace, strife, contention, debate, murmur, grudge, riches, poverty, penury, truth, falsehood, justice, equity, deceit, oppression, magnanimity, activity, force, attempraunce, treason, murder, felony . . . and also how a commonwealth might be edified and also continued within our realm. Howbeit, in conclusion, we have done as our predecessors have been wont to do, that is to say, as well as we might, and left where we began.

In 1515 the preamble to an Act passed to check absenteesism complained that important parliamentary business was 'greatly delayed', because '. . . . divers knights of shires, citizens for cities, burgesses for boroughs, and barons of the Cinque Ports, long time before the end of the said Parliament of their own authority depart and goeth home to their counties'. Therefore, the Act prescribed that, in future, a member should not absent himself 'till the same Parliament be fully finished, ended or prorogued', although so that he might attend to 'his great business and affairs' a member could obtain a licence from the Speaker and the House, 'the same licence to be entered on record in the book of the clerk of the Parliament appointed . . . for the Commons' House'.

Still members absented themselves, and the loss of wages, included as a punishment in the Act, was hardly a deterrent. In Elizabeth's reign leaving the House, 'before the Speaker arise to go' – and he, poor man, has no choice but to attend every day – was punishable by a penalty of 4d (increased in 1589 to 6d) to be paid into the poor box.

No daily roll call was made when the House was sitting, certainly from Edward VI's reign, but a spot check could be made by 'calling the House' on the special summons of the Speaker. Then the roll of members' names was read from the Clerk's book. According to William Lambarde 'It is a common policy to say upon the Wednesday that the House shall be called on Saturday, and on Saturday to say it shall be called on Wednesday, and so from day to day, by fear thereof to keep the company together'.

Lawyers, of course, were the chief offenders, nipping out to attend 'their clients' causes and neglecting service of this House', but there were others too, who used their time in London to pursue their own business ventures, or who felt, as the Recorder of Beaumaris felt, that as 'one that loves to see fashions and desires to know wonders', participation in the social life of the capital was the chief perquisite of attendance in Parliament.

According to the division lists only 276 of a total membership of 411 attended the Parliament of 1563, 86 out of 462 the Parliament of 1589. Absentees in 1581 were fined at the rate of £20 for a county member, £10 for a borough member if they had missed the whole session, and the amount of the fine does not belittle the problem; small wonder that a committee was set up in 1589 to deal with the whole problem, yet nothing seems to have resulted from its deliberations.

The problem continued into the seventeenth century, and afternoon sittings of the House did not help; on one occasion when but 20 members and the Speaker met for an afternoon sitting, there were only 17 members when the House reassembed the next morning. The highest number of members attending the House in James I's reign was about 330, but this was a figure only rarely approached; as the session progressed attendance dropped, so that a mere 100 or less remained at the end.

The conclusion we must draw is that the work of the House of Commons was really done by a solid core of some 60 to 80 M.P.s, and small groupings of these, like the Puritan kernel of parliamentary nuisances, described in a lampoon of 1566 as the 'choir', compared to which the remainder were but a parrot-like chorus.

[3] PARLIAMENTARY REPRESENTATION

Local government

Sixteenth-century Englishmen, like their medieval ancestors, thought of society in terms of communities – the county, the borough; to them it was quite natural that parliamentary representation should be based upon those communities, and they would never have understood our modern view that representation should be proportioned to population. In a predominantly agricultural society the possession of land was the test of wealth, of social status and political influence, and the owners of land – the landed gentry – constituted, by natural right, the ruling class of that society. Therefore, the counties and the country gentry, the accepted leaders of their communities and their independent and vigorous representatives in Parliament, were the most important element in Tudor politics. And here was a situation the exact reverse of the pattern of continental politics where the Court and not the localities was the centre of political life.

The counties were governed by officials, for the most part unsalaried. These were the Lords Lieutenant and their deputies in each shire, the Sheriffs, and the Justices of the Peace. They were all essentially county men, educated together in their county grammar schools and, in all probability, at one or other of the universities. More often than not they did not take their degrees, but moved on to what Sir John Neale has called those 'finishing schools for gentlemen' the Inns of Court; here they acquired a knowledge of the law, and, as it would serve their ambition, a liking for it; it would, as Fuller wrote, 'help him to keep his own, and bestead his neighbours'.

Lords Lieutenant

The office of Lord Lieutenant was a Tudor creation, and although it could be held by a commoner it was more usually occupied by the chief nobleman of the county who had close connections with the Court. Sometimes his responsibility extended over more than one shire, and when this was so the effective duties of the office were more often performed by his deputies, two or more, chosen from among the most influential of the country gentlemen. Primarily the Lord Lieutenant was military leader of the shire, his main duty being to hold the annual shire musters and to see that the militia, which he commanded, and on whom the country's defence depended, were properly mustered and equipped. Not unnaturally he acquired other duties too, like the implementation of government economic legislation and the administration of taxation and enforcement of religious uniformity.

Sheriffs

Since their implication with noble families during the Wars of the Roses, the authority of the Sheriffs, which had once been supreme in the counties, had been greatly curtailed, and many of the duties that they had performed had been progressively transferred to the Justices of the Peace. The Sheriff's office had become a 'burdensome and expensive honour, only to be borne because it lasted only a year and came but once in a gentleman's life' (Elton); nevertheless, they still held some administrative authority, especially in the supervision of parliamentary elections on which they continued to exercise a great deal of influence.

Justices of the Peace

The Justices of the Peace, a well-tried medieval institution, saw their powers extended during the Tudor period, much of the work formerly done by the Sheriffs being transferred to them. Their main business remained the preservation of order, and in this they were Henry VII's main agents, being granted wide powers to check livery and maintenance, and, in 1495, the power to punish Sheriffs and Bailiffs found guilty of extortion. At Petty Sessions two or three J.P.s sitting together could deal with certain less important misdemeanours, while in the General Sessions, held at least four times a year, they could try any indictable offence except treason. In addition they dealt with matters of vagabondage, agriculture and industry, and, as their authority grew, they came more and more under the control of the King and his Privy Council. Their authority extended only to the limits of their own shires, they held office for one year, and received payment at the rate of 4/- a day for their work at the Sessions.

County members

The country gentleman was thus accustomed to exercising authority and influence and arousing deference within his shire neighbourhood, and when he sat in Parliament at Westminster he expected that his status should arouse a similar respect. To be elected to sit as knight of the shire was a coveted honour to be enjoyed by just a few of the most prominent county families, and foreigners were generally excluded.

It was a matter of prestige, too, to be returned as the 'first', or senior of the two knights of the shire, as more honour was attached to the senior position even though there may have been only two candidates for the two places. The rules of the game were really enforced by the ideas of degree and precedence; certainly the county seats should go to county families, and wherever possible this should be arranged and agreed upon rather than fought for, because a disputed election was a social and financial catastrophe and a sure indication that ever-present faction had got out of hand and was threatening to disrupt the established order in the county. Defeat in an election dealt such an ineradicable blow to the pride and prestige of the loser that his whole standing in the county was in danger, and he might well feel that the only honourable course open to him was to leave the county altogether and live on some other of his estates. This was why the majority of Elizabethan county elections were not contested but were a foregone conclusion, for if 'having the repulse' was at all likely a gentleman just would not risk it.

A statute of 1445 stipulated that the representatives of the counties were to be 'notable knights of the same counties for the which they shall be chosen, or otherwise such notable esquires,

gentlemen of birth of the same counties as shall be able to be
knights; and no man to be such knight which standeth in the
degree of a yeoman and under'. In effect this imposed a property
qualification of £20, as ownership of property to that annual
value was the essential prerequisite for knighthood.

County franchise

Until 1430 all freeholders in the county could vote at the election of the knight of the shire, but then the forty-shilling freehold qualification was fixed by statute. Roughly, this meant
that the vote was exercised by the 'yeomanry', which included
anyone who owned his own farm, and also a number of substantial tenant farmers on copyhold. It was easy to become a gentleman from being an independent farmer, and it may be that in
the poorer parts of the country there was hardly any significant
distinction. But they were still expected to do their feudal duty
and vote for their own lord; it would have been considered a grave
breach of faith in most cases to have done otherwise.

County election

Just as soon as it became known that a new Parliament was to
be summoned the machinery was set on foot in the counties to
provide suitable and acceptable candidates. Those who were
socially eligible would begin casting about among their friends
for support, or it may have been simply a case of a powerful
local person, or alliance of personages, informing the Sheriff,
to whom the election writs were sent, of their desired choice as
representatives.

The election was held at the county court, which met every
fourth week in the county town, and the Sheriff or his deputy
presided. In the Elizabethan period the actual election proceedings were supposed to begin between 8 and 9 in the morning,
although the statute of 1430 specified between 8 and 11.

In large counties like Yorkshire the freeholders had to travel considerable distances to exercise their voting right, and were bound to stay overnight in the county town, so rival factions would take over the local inns to house their supporters, or potential supporters.

When the crowd of freeholders assembled (in the Yorkshire election in 1597 about 6,000 were present) the court was proclaimed, the election writ read out and the election followed. Candidates were usually nominated by the Justices of the Peace and leading gentlemen of the shire who sat with the Sheriff on the bench. When the names were put to the freeholders voting was by acclamation, and when he considered the shouting had gone on long enough the Sheriff gave his verdict.

If his verdict was challenged the Sheriff might then either take a 'view', which was done by dividing the supporters of the various candidates, then guessing their relative numbers, or a 'poll' would be taken. When this happened the electors passed before the Sheriff and representatives of the candidates to be counted. If an elector's qualifications to vote were questioned an oath sworn on the Holy Evangelist that his freehold was indeed worth forty shillings or more had to be taken; doubtful cases were closely examined, and perjury could be punished by Star Chamber. When all had been counted the Sheriff declared the final result and made his return into Chancery.

This poll, because of the numbers involved and the doubtful enthusiasm of the Sheriff for a speedy decision, could be a long drawn out affair, and the Montgomeryshire election in 1588, which began at 8 o'clock on the Saturday morning, dragged through all that day and night and was not finally resolved until about 5 o'clock on the Sunday morning.

The role of the Sheriff

Now the key figure in all these proceedings was the Sheriff. He was in charge of the arrangements for, and conduct of, the election; he was also the returning officer. Very rarely was the Sheriff impartial; indeed, he commonly rigged the whole business, for being a leading county man himself he was likely to be mixed up in local faction, and his own friends might well be candidates.

Various devices were used to bring about the required result. In 1593 the Sheriff of Nottinghamshire adjourned 'the county court from the Shire Hall within the town to Her Majesty's Castle' outside it, so that while the Earl of Shrewsbury's nominees were being returned the rival candidates were left kicking their heels in the Shire Hall.

The Sheriff might also guide an election if, at a poll, he counted the freeholders supporting the favoured candidate first; then he could so slow down his counting that those freeholders ready to vote for the rival candidate got fed up with waiting and made their way home and never cast their vote. This was the misfortune of one of the candidates in the 1584 Hertfordshire election, who was sure that if his supporters had only been counted first 'it would have furthered us greatly'.

Once the writ for calling a new Parliament was received it was the Sheriff's duty to hold the election at the very next county court; often, however, the Sheriff would not disclose that a writ had actually been received until the favoured candidate, with whom he did share his information, had got himself and his supporters organized, and his opponents were then caught almost entirely unawares and unprepared. Most blatant of all, the Sheriff could falsify his return to Chancery, as did the Sheriff in the 1559 Wiltshire election, who actually reversed the result of the poll in making his return.

A statute of 1429 had imposed a £100 fine and a year's imprisonment on any Sheriff guilty of misconducting an election, and this was confirmed by another statute, in 1445, which further allowed a wronged candidate to bring an action for debt for £100 against the offending Sheriff. Such an action was in fact brought in Mary's reign, but by Elizabeth's reign the financial deterrent was no longer effective as rapid inflation had reduced its value. The candidate who suborned a Sheriff by guaranteeing to pay his fine if he would only put his name on the return, knew this well: the Sheriff 'might return whom he would . . . notwithstanding he were never elected, for . . . he knew the Sheriff did for such offence incur but the penalty of one hundred pounds', which he 'was well able to pay' (Neale).

In Elizabeth's reign election cases were tried in Star Chamber, but even if a Sheriff was fined this was only done when his return was displeasing to the Queen and her ministers, and in any case the Court could not unseat a member, even if he had been fraudulently elected, because too long a time elapsed between the making of the complaint and the giving of the Court's judgment. In the reign of James I such matters arising from elections were dealt with by the House of Commons itself.

Sometimes a county seat was contested, and then the interloper would make contact, first with the gentry of the shire to gain their support and, through them, perhaps, the support of their tenants and other freeholders, or directly by bribery and intrigue, means which were being used at county elections as early as 1467. At such times the county might well become 'too much wrought into faction', as indeed was the county of Norfolk in the election of 1601, following on a threatened duel, which followed a real one in the previous year, and which foreshadowed the taking of sides in Essex's abortive rebellion. Generally, however, as there were no party politics in the Tudor period, there was not really a choice of candidates as knights of the shire, and the ambitious country gentry, thwarted in this direction, looked to the boroughs to provide their entry into the House of Commons. The process had begun in the fifteenth century, but with some difficulty the Crown had been able to hold it in check; in the Tudor period, however, it could be restrained no longer, and the clamour of the country gentlemen could only be satisfied by the creation, as we have seen, of more and more parliamentary boroughs.

Borough franchise

A resolution of the Parliamentary Committee of Privileges of 1628 clearly stated the 'the election of burgesses in all boroughs did of common right belong to the commoners, and that nothing could take it away from them but a prescription and a constant usage beyond all memory to the contrary'. Probably the borough franchise was once in the hands of all the burgesses, that is the free inhabitants of the borough, householders paying scot and lot (i.e. they were liable for taxes demanded for local or national purposes) who did not live by wages, or by an innkeeper, butcher, brewer, or baker, and were enrolled at the Court Leet. But in the fourteenth century votes were not yet of value, seats in the House of Commons not yet in so great a demand, and, as a result, municipal corporations fell into the habit of taking over the election of the borough representatives with little or no reference to the townspeople; and the townspeople often encouraged the process by waiving their own right of election, or by delegating that right to the rapidly closing corporations. Royal charters of incorporation from Henry VI's reign onwards accepted this situation and granted the new corporations the election of their members of Parliament – 'the later the charter the more oligarchic is the constitution of the borough' (F. W. Maitland in *Township and Borough*, Cambridge University Press, 1898).

An Act of 1444 declared that elections were to be made by the citizens and burgesses; but it was impossible to put the clock back, and the close corporations refused to share their acquired privilege to the very end of their existence in 1835. If justification of their position was necessary then they claimed, as they did in the Stuart period, that were elections to be shared with the town inhabitants 'popular tumults' would be the result at election time.

There was, however, no uniformity in the borough franchise. If most borough M.P.s were returned on a corporation vote and a mere handful of electors, some entered the Commons on a freeman vote, all freemen voting, as at Coventry, which had 600 electors in 1628; a burgage tenure vote, as in the manorial borough of Bletchingly in Surrey; or on a resident burgess vote, as at Shrewsbury with an electorate of some 420. Newton in Lancashire, enfranchised in 1558, was unique in that it was the only English borough in which the forty-shilling freehold franchise was the sole qualification for the vote.

The franchise in the Welsh boroughs, included in the parliamentary system in 1536, was on a popular basis, established as it was according to the existing English system, that is to say the forty-shilling freehold franchise. This meant that their electorates were large, and this and the fact that the electors were widely scattered because of the amalgamation of boroughs made the Welsh boroughs less vulnerable than their English counterparts to outside influence and control by borough patrons.

Wages of Members

In the Middle Ages M.P.s had been paid wages by their con-stituencies: 4/- a day for county members, 2/- for borough mem-bers during the Parliamentary session and covering travelling time to and from Westminster, for which they might also receive a travelling allowance on the basis of a day's journey of 20 miles in winter and 30 in summer. By the sixteenth century many M.P.s had made written agreements with their constituencies for a payment either above or below the statutory rate, and increasing-ly for no payment at all, so anxious were they to serve in Parlia-ment.

The last legal recognition of wages for M.P.s was contained in the 1554 statute, which applied the English scale of pay to the new Welsh constituencies, but generally by 1547 M.P.s had ceased to claim wages, although many boroughs made voluntary pay-ments. London paid its four M.P.s a wage and provided them with a clothing allowance, attendants, and a special allowance of 4/- a day for a senior member, 2/- for a junior if Parliament was held outside London. From 1571 to 1587 London M.P.s were also allowed 1/- a day for boat hire, while in 1581 each was provided with a scarlet gown for each session, or £6 13 4 instead.

County gentlemen and borough representation

But many boroughs found payment of their representatives' wages a heavy burden – the eight sessions of the 'Reformation

Parliament', for example, must have entailed very heavy bills for members' wages for many boroughs – and so they welcomed a man who was prepared to serve them gratuitously, just as they welcomed a patron, often a neighbouring country gentleman, usually High Steward for the borough, who was prepared to organize everything and to afford them his help and protection, by representing their interests in London, or at the Court. Thus financial considerations speeded up the process of returning members of the country gentry as M.P.s for boroughs; small boroughs no longer had any reason to fear being enfranchised, and the creation of parliamentary boroughs, as we have seen, increased rapidly as the Crown reluctantly submitted to the threefold pressure of borough patron, borough, and country gentry.

So the legislation of 1413, 1429, 1432 and 1445 that required knights and burgesses to be 'dwelling and resident' within the constituency they represented was flagrantly broken, and before the end of the sixteenth century had fallen into disuse, even though it was not repealed until 1774. Had this legislation been obeyed the House of Commons in late Elizabethan times ought to have consisted of 90 country gentlemen and 372 burgesses and townsmen; in fact the proportion of gentlemen to townsmen was reversed, and in Elizabeth's House of Commons at the end of her reign there were at least four country gentlemen to every townsman. 'The country gentleman and his cousin, the lawyer,' writes Sir John Neale, 'had captured the House of Commons.'

Nevertheless, the House of Commons gained immeasurably from this development. These new borough members did not represent narrow local interests as the townsmen might well have done, but were men of considerable social standing, self-reliant men of affairs, who moved about the country, and whose experience in local administration, and, above all, whose training in the Common Law made them a most formidable element in Parliament. Here were no potential royal 'yes-men'; without them the House of Commons could not have stood up to the Lords, much less challenged the Crown, and Charles I would not have suffered death in 1649.

Some few boroughs, however, remained independent of the percolating gentry and returned what may be termed 'old-style' M.P.s, that is local tradesmen or merchants; or they may have compromised by electing one local man with one outsider. London returned four M.P.s – all citizens, but then the larger boroughs were better able to resist outside influence in their affairs, and they could afford to be independent. Yet even they were caught by the rising gentry tide. The only boroughs which remained independent throughout Elizabeth's reign were Bristol, Bath, Ludlow and Worcester; York held out until 1601, and Salisbury succumbed only once – in 1572 – but then the city authorities made it quite clear that they had no intention of making a habit of it.

It is important to appreciate the position of the borough vis-à-vis its M.P. By his willingness to forgo wages and expenses the member had ingratiated himself with the municipal authority; but it was the borough that was bestowing the favour, and the member had to keep on the right side of the municipal authority, or this favour might well be transferred elsewhere.

There are grounds for supposing that from James I's reign boroughs were demanding 'something for the corporation' as a reasonable return from a member for his election, and in the reign of his son matters had reached the point where constituencies began to expect, indeed to demand, that those who sought their suffrages should also bear some of the charges for municipal undertakings, which ought properly to have been charges borne by the community as a whole.

Not until 1835 were the close corporations destroyed, just three years after the first tangible measure of parliamentary reform. But ideas of electoral reform were in the air in the Tudor period. In 1628 the wheel came full circle when electoral rights were restored to 'the common sort of Burgesses' at Boston, Bridport, Colchester, Lewes, and Warwick, and the municipal oligarchies in these boroughs were deprived of the exclusive right of electing M.P.s. Popular movements within the boroughs for a restitution of wider parliamentary franchises were helped forward by the work of the Parliamentary Committee of Privileges of 1628, and its effects were seen in the later Stuart period in 1660 and 1688.

Restrictions on candidature

Finally, what restrictions, if any, were there on a constituency's choice of an M.P.? As we have seen, a definite legal restriction (1445) of county representation to knights, or persons fit for knighthood, as opposed to yeomen, ruled out those not holding land of the value of £20 a year. For the boroughs, their own mayors, clergymen, peers, infants, men of unsound mind, and aliens were ineligible.

In 1547 a law of 1372, re-enacted in 1532 and which excluded Sheriffs from sitting in the House of Commons, was made to apply to the mayors of boroughs. But the law was never quite clear on this point, and the matter was raised in 1604 by an M.P., who asked 'to know the opinion of the House, whether the mayor of a town might be lawfully returned and admitted to serve as a member here'. Obviously it was a moot point; for a mayor, to whom election writs for the boroughs were directed, could easily contrive his own election, and yet if he was fairly elected for a borough other than his own no objection should be raised. The House finally resolved that if a mayor was chosen for a county then he could serve, but he could not sit as a burgess.

Clergymen, because they were represented in Convocation and taxed by Convocation from 1553, could neither vote nor be elected to Parliament. They did not assume the privilege of voting for the return of M.P.s until 1664, but from 1407 they were barred from sitting as M.P.s; and, although there are three recorded cases of clergymen being elected between the reign of Mary Tudor and the Restoration, they were not allowed to serve.

Although peers were, and are, ineligible to sit in the House of Commons the early usage that also excluded the eldest sons of peers broke down in 1549, when Sir Francis Russell, then M.P. for Tavistock, became heir-apparent to the Earl of Bedford. He was allowed to continue in the House, as indeed was his son, a burgess for Bridport in 1575. From then on the House of Commons spoilt the eldest sons of peers rather, and allowed them to sit with the Privy Councillors on the cross-benches to the right of the Speaker's chair. There sat Denzil Holles, 'being entitled to it as an Earl's son, when he and Valentine manhandled the Speaker in 1629.

[4] PATRONAGE

The web of patronage

On All Hallows Day 1529, George Cavendish, Wolsey's gentleman-usher, found another of the Cardinal's servants, Thomas Cromwell, taking stock of his own position now that his master's world had crumbled into enforced retirement at Esher. An ambitious man, Cromwell well knew that success in Tudor times came, as it had done in the previous century, to the man who secured the patronage of some magnate of the realm, best of all now the King, to be his 'good lord'. Therefore, he told Cavendish, 'I will this afternoon . . . ride to London, and to the Court, when I will either make or mar, ere ever I come again'.

Within a few days he had returned, and his 'pleasant countenance' revealed that his journey had prospered, for he had 'put his feet where he would be better regarded, ere ever the Parliament was finished'. With the approval of the King and the Duke of Norfolk, and through the good offices of another former servant of the shattered Cardinal, Sir William Paulet, Cromwell sat as a member for Taunton in the first session of the Reformation Parliament. Now, with the right influence and connections the ladder of advancement might well become an escalator. Our Tudor ancestors could be as critical of patronage as we are, but, like us, they could not manage without it; the struggle for prestige, and the social and financial perquisites that went with it, dominated English political life.

Sir John Neale has vividly described the Elizabethan political scene. At the centre of the web of politics and patronage was the Queen, the source of all power, the cynosure of all men's eyes and of the poets' art, and the Court. About her were her ministers, 'never more than tenants-at-will', according to a contemporary, and as the Queen could not herself operate the whole elaborate system of patronage single-handed she allowed it to be diffused through her ministers. Yet still she remained in control by preserving delicately, if at times precariously, the balance of faction – the party politics of the sixteenth century.

All through the earlier Tudor period there were fierce faction fights for power and prestige, as well as personal and family feuds – *Romeo and Juliet* could be appreciated and understood as a play about factional hatreds. These contests, especially in the more remote regions of the country, had more often than not been settled by force and bloodshed, but under Elizabeth such rivalries were brought within the framework of the law by having recourse to litigation, and in this the Court of Star Chamber had played an invaluable part.

Almost every county had its factions and this situation was reflected in the Court factions of the time, except in the capital where local feuds and local style quarrels were reproduced on a larger and politically more significant scale. It was the political manoeuvre of Elizabeth to play off one against the other. 'The principal note of her reign', wrote Sir Robert Naunton, 'will be that she ruled much by faction and parties which she herself both made, upheld and weakened, as her own great judgment advised'; and, in the opinion of Sir Henry Wotton, this 'was not the least ground of much of her quiet and success'. Had any one faction succeeded in coming out on top it would have resulted in political catastrophe.

It suited both the interest and the disposition of the Queen to have these factions competing for her favours, but influence alone was insufficient recommendation for one of her ministers; she had no intention of allowing the wrong man into office, and first made enquiries about him, referring constantly to Burghley who, although he was not much better than his contemporaries in that he, too, 'grew rich' from gratuities, was nevertheless not open to bribery, and his advice was, at all times, sincere and un-prompted by a hankering after financial reward.

There were, however, 'some of the Queen's Council that were not in the catalogue of saints.'. But then holding office under the Crown bought in very little by way of a direct income; for the Queen's revenue would not allow her to pay her officials ade-quately, and most Crown posts in the counties were virtually unsalaried, since they depended for their origins on the medieval system of landholding with service. Office-holders, therefore, ministers and minor officials alike, battened on to the inestimable benefits of patronage to lead them on to fortune and prosperity, and the greater the office, the higher the standing at Court, the more patronage it was possible to command. Members of the Court inner circle, those with access to the privy chamber – statesmen, courtiers and ladies of the Court – sold their favours among the multitude of suitors who thronged the Court and who had already oiled the wheels of favour by tipping still more members of the patronage pyramid – the secretaries, the clerks (many of them the younger sons of country gentry intent on finding their fortunes in 'the gentlemanly profession of serving men'), the very porter at the door; 'For nothing there is done without a fee: the courtier needs must recompensed be.'

The insatiable appetite for favours was such a cutthroat busi-ness that by no means all who tried were successful in climbing aboard the patronage band-wagon. Many smarted in the political wilderness; Sir Walter Raleigh, for example, because the Queen did not trust him, and Francis Bacon who, in supporting Essex, backed the wrong horse.

If being on the spot at Court was no guarantee of success, then absence from it spelled inevitable failure, particularly for the faction leaders. The Earl of Leicester wrote to Sir Francis Wal-singham from the Netherlands: 'I pray you to stand fast for your poor absent friends against calumniators', but he was too far away to prevent Burghley appointing three of Leicester's politi-cal opponents – Whitgift, Cobham and Buckhurst – to the Privy Council.

Absence from the Court was also disastrous for the politically inept Earl of Essex, for at these times his rival, Robert Cecil, had become Secretary, Chancellor of the Duchy of Lancaster and Master of the Court of Wards – an office greatly coveted and long angled for by Essex. 'I am not ignorant', he wrote on 4 January 1599 on his unlooked for appointment as commander-in-chief in Ireland, 'what are the disadvantages of absence; the opportunities of practising enemies when they are neither encountered nor overlooked.' His thoughts were no less gloomy in a later letter: 'I provided for this service a breastplate and not a cuirass; that is, I am armed on the breast but not on the back.'

Obviously there were many dangers inherent in a system of government based on patronage and where 'it is not the use in any place . . . to do good turns gratis'. Gratuities could so easily become unashamed bribes, and this, in fact, had happened by the last decade of Elizabeth's reign. 'I will forbear', wrote one of Burghley's supporters, 'to mention the great and unusual fees exacted lately by reason of buying and selling offices, both judicial and ministerial, as also the privileges granted private persons to the great prejudice and grievance of the common people.'

Faction rivalry at Court, balanced for so long by the Queen, could also get out of hand and threaten the whole stability of the State, and this too was happening when Elizabeth recoiled from the violence of Essex and supported just one faction, the Cecilians. The men of the 1590s were out of tune with the old ways and days, out of tune with the Queen – and she knew it: 'Now', she said to the antiquary Lambarde in 1601, 'the wit of the fox is everywhere on foot, so as hardly a faithful or virtuous man may be found.' Certainly Burghley himself was not entirely immune to corruption in his last years, and his son was always ready to exploit the opportunities for patronage provided by his offices. Rising inflation, coupled with the poverty of the Crown and James I's political and personal weaknesses (not least his habitual inability to distinguish a wise man from a fool) saw the complete collapse of the Elizabethan political system in the early years of the seventeenth century.

Political patronage

A seat in the House of Commons, as Thomas Cromwell well knew, provided an ambitious man with an entrée to the labyrinth of Court patronage with a fair chance later (as his own career was to demonstrate most clearly) to influence, or control some of that patronage himself. Patronage had secured his election for the borough of Taunton in 1529 and, by patronage, local pressures, sometimes by downright jobbery, the members for the shires and boroughs were regularly returned. Despite the decline in the importance of the House of Lords in the Tudor period many illustrious noblemen, like the Earls of Bedford, Rutland, and Northamptonshire, and the Dukes of Norfolk, continued to exercise a tremendous influence on local government and all appointments to office, as they still regarded themselves virtually absolute in their own areas.

These members of local territorial families and powerful courtiers also obtained and exercised borough patronage, although the term 'borough patron' belongs to the eighteenth century and would not have been used in the Tudor and Stuart periods. The Tudor patron indeed was still dependent upon the goodwill of the boroughs, and his letters to them are generally couched in restrained terms, seeking favours rather than issuing instructions; and in Parliament and at Court they supported the interests of the boroughs to which he had attached himself, as High Steward perhaps, or as Recorder.

Borough patronage was, therefore, mutually beneficial to the borough and the patron. Thomas Denton of Buckinghamshire, who, by his 'labor and delygent Sewte' had assisted in securing the borough's first Charter in 1554, sat as Banbury's first Member of Parliament. Sir George Carey, because at his 'special instance . . . two burgesses were admitted into the High Court of Parliament' in 1584 for Newport, Isle of Wight, was granted in gratitude by the borough for life the right to nominate one of the two burgesses. He had doubtless performed a like service for two other Isle of Wight boroughs enfranchised in 1584, because in 1601 he wrote to the Mayor and burgesses of Yarmouth: 'Send up unto me (as heretofore you have done) your writ, with a blank wherein I may insert the names of such persons as I shall think fittest to discharge that duty for your behoof'.

Here we can see clearly the making of 'pocket' boroughs, which had acquired such notoriety by 1830; and in Aylesbury we can see a pocket borough already notorious in the reign of Elizabeth. Aylesbury had been enfranchised by charter in 1554 and was firmly in the hands of the Packington family of Worcestershire. Dame Dorothy Packington, lord of the borough, in her election return of 1572 made no bones of the fact that the two members for the borough owed their nomination to her:

Know ye, me, the said Dame Dorothy Packington, to have chosen, named, and appointed my trusty and well-beloved Thomas Lichfield and George Burden esquires to be my burgesses of my said town of Aylesbury. And whatsoever the said Thomas and George, burgesses, shall do in the service of the Queen's Highness in that present parliament to be holden at Westminster ... I, the same Dame Dorothy Packington, do ratify and approve to be my own act, as fully and wholly as if I were or might be present there.

This forthright and brazen example was followed by her son, John, and the election precept in 1586 and 1597 was actually addressed to him, not, as the law required it should have been, to the bailiff.

Most boroughs had a High Steward, and his function was to be their patron and protector, and a good choice was a courtier to ensure they had a friend at Court, for their own local needs and wishes outweighed any concern they might feel for national interests. For their part courtiers were eager to accept such offers, indeed they may well have competed with one another to get them. For the patron, not only did a High Stewardship involve the payment of some fee (which was always welcome) – £4 a year perhaps, as at Nottingham, or £10 a year as at Ipswich and Plymouth – but more than that it gave a courtier, vis-à-vis his political rivals, added prestige and power. For the borough, too, it was a matter of considerable prestige if their High Steward and patron at Court was Lord Burghley, Sir Francis Walsingham, Sir Robert Cecil, or the leading royal favourite.

Great patrons: Leicester, Burghley, Essex, Robert Cecil

The Earl of Essex was an inveterate patron, and both he and the
Earl of Leicester held many High Stewardships. Leicester, 'this
supreme patron of high Elizabethan days' (Neale), was High
Steward of Andover, Bristol, Reading, Wallingford, Great Yarmouth, King's Lynn and probably Gloucester; Steward at
Abingdon and New Windsor, and Recorder of Maldon. Even so
his parliamentary patronage within these boroughs was not
especially successful; his nominations for Parliament cut very
little ice with Reading, Great Yarmouth, or King's Lynn; or
with Maldon, where the Earl of Essex interjected a rival interest.
Nevertheless, his control of Abingdon was secure until he resigned
his High Stewardship in 1580, and certainly six – probably many
more – of the members of the 1584 Parliament were Leicester's
nominees.

Essex's star was not yet in the ascendant in 1588 when Leicester died, and it was Burghley who succeeded Leicester as High
Steward of Bristol and Great Yarmouth. With his death, however, ten years later, the last of the great Elizabethan statesmen
disappeared from the scene to follow men like Sir Christopher
Hatton, Sir Francis Knollys, Sir Francis Walsingham, and the
Earls of Bedford, Huntingdon and Shrewsbury. The way was
now open for lesser men to debase the moral standards of the
time by their own ambitious pursuit of influence and power. The
vainglorious Essex and the lesser Cecil – 'Robert le Diable' –
stood as prime combatants, each fostering activities that were
the very antithesis of Elizabethan practice; by consciously
attempting to secure a party in the House of Commons they un-
consciously cleared the way for the jobbery and corruption that
were to be released in English political life in the early part of the
seventeenth century.

By 1598 Essex had been chosen as their High Steward by
Ipswich, Bristol, Great Yarmouth, St Albans, Cambridge, (where
he had succeeded Burghley), Andover, Dunwich, Hereford,
Leominster, Tamworth, Oxford and Reading. In Staffordshire
his influence was most active, and here in 1593 he tried to secure

a monopoly of all the county's parliamentary seats; six of the county's ten seats were filled by his nominees. Members for Dunwich, Reading, Shaftesbury, Shrewsbury, Radnor, Cardigan and Carmarthen returned to the same Parliament were also nominees of Essex.

For his part Robert Cecil attempted to outdo Essex in getting his own supporters into Parliament, and he was a formidable opponent. Besides the influence available to him as High Steward of Doncaster, Hull, Plymouth and Westminster, and as Recorder of Colchester, his sudden appointment by the Queen as Chancellor of the Duchy of Lancaster in 1597, when the Essex faction was weakened by their leader's absence on the unsuccessful Island's Voyage, greatly increased his patronage and his opportunities for influencing elections.

His appointment as Master of the Court of Wards in 1599 meant that he had to resign the Duchy, but he continued with his political tactic of securing the transfer of parliamentary nominations from other borough patrons to himself. Undoubtedly Essex got the worst of the power struggle with Cecil, but not all of the boroughs were impressed by the Secretary's performance (his conduct in the trial and execution of Essex in 1601 in particular), and demonstrated the fact that even at the beginning of the seventeenth century they could still retain something of their independance. Cecil was not invited to take Essex's place as High Steward of Great Yarmouth, Ipswich, Bristol, or Oxford, and at Reading his nomination for the office was actually defeated.

Ports and the Cinque ports

The ports, being very cosmopolitan, were particularly susceptible to the return of outsiders as their members of Parliament. In 1597 Southampton elected Francis Bacon, who appears to have had no link with the town at all, while Plymouth returned Henry Bromley, a gentleman of Worcestershire and Shropshire, to the Parliaments of 1584 and 1586, and Miles Sandys of Buckinghamshire to that of 1588.

Ipswich and Portsmouth were equally amenable to outside guidance, and Chichester returned the nominee of Lord Lumley, their High Steward, William Ashbie, 'a mere stranger unto this place, and unknown to us all, and only liked and allowed of by your Lordship's commendations'. One notable exception to this pattern was Great Yarmouth, which consistently elected its own townsmen and set at nought the wishes of an impressive list of powerful patrons, including the Earl of Leicester, Lord Burghley and the Earl of Essex.

The Cinque Ports – Sandwich, Dover, Hythe, Romney, Rye, Winchelsea and Hastings – were a special case as the Lord Warden, to whom writs for parliamentary elections were addressed and through whom returns were made, was clearly able to exercise parliamentary patronage in the selection of the two 'barons' returned by each of the ports. His success fluctuated, however, as there was a strong spirit of independence among the ports. In 1572 Rye, Romney and Hythe resisted the Warden's influence and chose local men, as did Rye again and Sandwich in 1584.

The tenth Lord Cobham, Warden of the Cinque Ports for most of Elizabeth's reign, had claimed in 1574 that he had the right to nominate one of the 'barons' in each of the seven ports, but such a claim was resisted by the ports themselves until, in 1614, the Lord Warden had come to regard it as 'the ancient usage and privilege that myself and my predecessors have ever had'. The claim had extended to the nomination of all fourteen barons by 1624, but the ports' independence was restored by an Act of 1689, which declared 'the right and freedom of election of members to serve in parliament for the Cinque Ports'.

One final point may be mentioned: a Leicestershire gentleman, Thomas Beaumont, was rejected as one of its burgesses by the borough of Leicester in 1597 on the justifiable grounds that he was 'an encloser himself and unlikely to redress that wrong in others', but such an exercise of political judgment in choosing a member of Parliament was, in the Tudor period, extremely rare.

Members and their constituencies

The relationship between a Member of Parliament and his constituency had been very close in the fourteenth century, but this did not last through the Tudor period. In 1339 the Commons had refrained from granting Edward III a large subsidy 'without consulting the commons of their countries', and it was 1340 before they agreed to the grant. Also, while wages were still being paid members usually reported back to their constituencies when, at the end of a Parliament, they put in their claims for wages and expenses; in 1524, for example, at Coventry, 'Mr Recorder related the Acts and manner of the last Parliament as a burgess of the city, and had hearty thanks therefore'.

As the constituencies' inability (or unwillingness) to pay their members' wages encouraged the drift into patronage the relationship of a member to his constituency became much more remote. Sometimes extra-parliamentary duties required by the House of Commons brought members into direct contact with their constituents. To ensure 'that one measure and one weight should be used throughout this noble realm', members were required to disperse to their constituencies at the end of the 1495 Parliament, and 'one of every weight and measure which now our Sovereign Lord hath caused to be made of brass', was to be sent to the town, city, or county town where the member was elected and there checked.

In 1624, and again in 1641, members were required to report on those recusants 'as are in places of charge or trust in their several counties and boroughs'. The fulfilment of such commissions was not difficult for knights who resided in their own shires but the growing number of non-resident borough members put up a very poor performance.

If the hold of a constituency on its members progressively relaxed, the House of Commons itself maintained an extremely tenacious hold over its members in the sixteenth and seventeenth centuries. A member could not resign his seat if his election had been against his own wishes, nor even if illness prevented his occupying it. 'A man after being duly chosen cannot refuse to

serve', decided the House in 1624 in the case of Sir Thomas
Escourt, who had been elected a knight for Gloucestershire
against his own consent and desire. The decision was thus explained: 'the county and commonwealth have such an interest
in every man, that when by lawful election he is appointed to
this public service, he cannot by any unwillingness and refusal of
his own make himself incapable, for that were to prefer the will
or contentment of a private man before the desire and satisfaction of the whole country, and a ready way to put by the suffi-
cientest men, who are commonly those who least endeavour to
obtain the place.'

Commons' membership: social classes

As we have already seen the largest single group of members of
the House of Commons was drawn from the landed classes, the
country gentlemen, whose numbers in the House increased as the
Tudor period progressed; they made up over half of the total
membership of the 1584 Parliament. The next largest group, certainly by Elizabeth's reign, were the Privy Councillors and royal
office-holders; their status and their administrative and political
experience made them an extremely important element, for men
like Thomas Cromwell and William Cecil were of their number.

But their presence in the Commons aroused frequent objec-
tions. One of the constitutional grievances expressed in the Pilgrimage of Grace in 1537 was that although 'the old custom was
that none of the king's servants should be of the common house;
yet most of that house were the king's servants'; while in 1555
an unsuccessful attempt was made to get a bill through Parliament to disqualify 'any stipendiary, pensioner or official, or any
person deriving profit in any other way from the King and royal
council, and being dependent on them'. The royal officials remained and accounted for about one-sixth of the membership of
the 1584 Parliament.

In this same Parliament, townsmen and businessmen, sent by
the merchant and trading cities and towns like London, Bristol,
Exeter, Hull, York and Barnstaple, and lawyers, were present in

equal numbers (fifty-three of each), but they were not of equal importance. The townsmen were outnumbered and outshone by the country gentlemen, although they were certainly not nonentities, for they always had their say when matters and bills affecting their mercantile interests were being debated; but the lawyers, by the nature of their profession, were outweighed by none.

The material benefits that resulted from the lawyer's membership of the House of Commons were considerable: on the floor of the House he could demonstrate his forensic skill and powers of oratory to attract more clients (in an age fascinated by litigation) and perhaps even to commend himself to the attention of the sovereign, or the sovereign's ministers. But, over and above this, his contribution to the development of Parliament was enormous. Bold and confident, he, with other university men, raised the standard of debate in the House of Commons; using his professional training he helped to elaborate parliamentary procedure; his skills were of value in framing bills, and parliamentary committees sometimes included 'all the lawyers of the house', so that his presence as a member established a strong link between the House of Commons and the Courts of Common Law – a powerful combination, as James I was later to discover to his cost.

The country gentry, besides invading the boroughs, had also invaded the universities and the Inns of Court, and this was reflected in the Commons' membership. Sir John Neale has given some figures for the Elizabethan Parliaments: in the 1563 Parliament, of the 420 members of the House of Commons 67 were university men (Cambridge, mostly) and 108 had studied at the Inns of Court. Of 460 members in the 1584 Parliament, 145 were university men, 164 were at the Inns of Court; and for the 1593 Parliament the numbers are 161 (most of them Oxford men) and 197.

If the academic training of members of the House of Commons was high, their great fund of practical experience was even more valuable. The Privy Councillors formed 'a managerial core', while the country gentry in their capacity as Justices of the Peace had acquired some considerable administrative experience in the running of their own county's affairs. But, above all, there was the steady acquisition of parliamentary experience. About

half of the members of an Elizabethan House of Commons had
served before, and some were very old hands at the game. Sir
Francis Knollys, for example, was a member of the Reformation
Parliament in 1534, probably sat in the remaining Parliaments
of Henry VIII's reign and the first of Mary's; he was in exile
until 1558, but then he sat in every Elizabethan Parliament
until his death in 1596. Moreover, he set an example to his family,
for a younger brother and five sons sat with him in the sessions
of 1576 and 1581. Indeed, it was not unusual to find several
members of one family sitting at the same time as members of
the Commons.

Parliamentary family connections

Often parliamentary families were related. Pollard noted the
considerable number of marriages which resulted from parliamentary connections, and saw the Reformation Parliament
particularly as something of a 'matrimonial agency'. 'But for
Parliamentary associations,' he wrote,

we should hardly expect to find Sir Edward Madison, M.P. for Hull,
marrying a sister of William Roper of Kent and M.P. for Bramber;
Roger Corbet of Moreton Corbet in Shropshire marrying a daughter of
Sir Andrew Windsor, M.P. for Berkshire, and sister of William Wind-
sor, M.P. for Wycombe; Henry Hussey, M.P. for Horsham, marrying
a daughter of Spring of Lavenham [Suffolk]; Reginald Littleprow,
M.P. for Norwich, marrying a Blount from Shropshire; Philip Barnard,
M.P. for Yarmouth, a Carew from Devon, and Charles Fox, M.P. for
Ludlow, a Crosby of Bury St Edmunds. Sir Nicholas Hare of Suffolk,
but M.P. for Downton [Wilts] in 1529 and Speaker in 1539, had three
sisters who apparently married respectively Reformation M.P.s for
Cambridge, Hindon, and Windsor.

There is sufficient evidence to show that this 'in-breeding' of
the parliamentary classes continued throughout the period.

Minors in Parliament

By parliamentary custom minors were excluded from membership of the House of Commons; nevertheless, over the whole

Tudor period they continued to sit. Edward Dudley was only seventeen when he represented Staffordshire in 1584, and another member of a prominent family, Charles Howard, sat for Bletchingly in 1597 at the age of nineteen. Minors had created something of a problem by 1613, when it was objected that no less than forty members of the House of Commons were 'not above twenty years of age, and some not exceeding sixteen', and one member complained that the session of 1621 'was pestered with the admission of so many young men; and that it was not fit they should make laws for the kingdom, who were not in their own persons liable to the law'. Not until late in the eighteenth century did minors disappear from Parliament, in spite of an Act against them in 1695.

The password to Parliament was certainly patronage; at Court and in the country, in the counties and the boroughs. But that is not the end of the story; there was increasing competition for seats, so that just knowing the right people was not necessarily enough – ability and merit were, in fact, tangible and essential assets. The Puritan diarist, Sir Simonds D'Ewes, makes this clear in his Journal. There were in the House of Commons, he writes 'many grave, many learned, many deep wise men, and those of ripe judgment'; they were indeed 'the flower and choice of the Realm'.

[5] OFFICERS OF PARLIAMENT

Chancellor Bishop Russell of Lincoln, in a sermon prepared for Edward V's first Parliament (which, in fact, never sat) compared the English constitution to that of Rome: 'the peuple [of Rome] . . . obteigned a specyalle magistrate called tribunus plebis to be their president in the consultacions, lyke as yn the senate the one of the consuls proposed and diffined alle that was amonges them . . . ; lyke as in this house [the Lords] one tanquam consul makithe the questions, soo yn the lower house in like wyse alle ys directed by the Speker quasi per tribunum'. Here, in 1483, were two parliamentary officers evidently discharging the functions of chairman – in the House of Lords the Chancellor, in the House of Commons the Speaker.

The Chancellor

The Chancellor, as the intermediary between the Crown and the Lords, had, in the fourteenth century, shared this role with the Chief Justice of the King's Bench and the Chamberlain, but before the end of the Tudor period his had become the major responsibility, and he had come to be called 'the Speaker of the higher house', or 'Lord Speaker', probably because his functions had become analagous to those of his opposite number in the Lower House.

The Speaker

From medieval times the primary function of the Speaker for the Commons had been to speak for them in the House of Lords. A medieval king summoning Parliament had certain demands to make of it and required answers to certain 'points' made in the 'charge' pronounced by the King, or his Chancellor at the opening of Parliament. The Commons, meeting independently of the Lords, then had to make their views known to the other House and the King. Sometimes this was done in writing, but more often orally, and here they chose someone to speak for them, a 'commune Parlour', a 'Prelocutor', or, the English equivalent, a 'Speaker'.

To begin with he was no more than casual spokesman for an ad hoc Commons' deputation, but from 1376 he was chosen by the Commons to act in their behalf, not for one occasion only, but for the duration of the parliamentary session.

These early Speakers were appointed for one year only, but many did not complete even that; frequently there were two Speakers in a year, in 1449 three. The position was an onerous and unpopular one and re-election was infrequent. Twice only in the Tudor period did the same Speaker preside in successive Parliaments: Sir John Baker in Henry VIII's last and Edward VI's first Parliament, and Sir John Puckering, Speaker in the Parliaments of 1585 and 1586. Not until the eighteenth century did it become customary to re-elect the Speaker.

It was as representative of the Commons that the Speaker acquired a distinctive status. But he was really a man of two worlds, for he was the servant of the Crown as well as of the Commons. Although in the first fifty years of the history of the Speakership the Commons were given a fairly free hand in expressing their own political independence by electing a Speaker of their own choice, almost all the medieval Speakers were men attached in some way to the Court – officers of the Royal Household, it may be, or members of the King's Council – so that their appointment as Speaker was almost a secondment.

The Speaker and the Crown

The Tudors were concerned to find a favourable Speaker at all times, and in the sixteenth century he was generally a government nominee, whose election by the Commons was a mere formality. There can be no doubt, for example, that Sir Thomas More's election as Speaker in 1523 had been arranged by the Lord Chancellor, for in complaining of More's failure to toe the required line, Wolsey petulantly remarked 'Would to God you had been at Rome, Master More, when I made you Speaker'.

Sir John Neale suggests that the election of a Speaker by the Elizabethan House of Commons was no more than a brief act of pantomime. The senior Privy Councillor present in the House nominated the government candidate, the House responding with murmurs of approval and acknowledging the election by a spattering of polite applause.

In 1566, after the death of the Speaker during a recess, the nomination of the official candidate, the Solicitor-General, Richard Onslow, was challenged and his election was carried on a division by only a narrow majority. But this was an isolated defiance; Crown employees continued as Speakers, and Sir John Eliot, writing in 1625 of the Speakership as then regarded by his fellow members in the Commons, described it as 'an office heretofore frequently filled by nullities, men selected for mere court convenience'.

Nevertheless, lip service was still paid, as late as 1571, to the principle of freedom from royal interference in the election of members of Parliament and Speaker alike, for John Hooker, in his *Order and Usage howe to keepe a Parliament*, published in that year, claimed 'that the King ought not to make any choice or cause anie choise to be made of any knight, cittizens, burgesses . . . [or] speaker of the common house . . .; but they must be elected and chosen by the laws, orders, and customs of the realm, as they were wont and ought to be'. His next clause, however – 'and the Kinges good advice yet not to be contemned' – gives the game away.

Not until 1679, when Sir Edward Seymour was re-elected Speaker in the face of Charles II's rejection, did the Commons assert their right to choose their own Speaker free of royal control; and not until the nineteenth century did the Speakership become a non-partisan office.

Election of a Speaker

The main procedural features for the election of the Speaker had emerged during the fifteenth century. First of all came the order to elect a Speaker, given to the Commons by the Chancellor, or, in his absence, by some other dignitary who had declared the causes of the assembly of Parliament. 'The use is (as in the congier de esleir of a bishop)' wrote a former Speaker, Sir Edward Coke, in his *Institutes*, 'that the King doth name a discreet and learned man whom the Commons elect.'

Then followed the Commons' presentation of their Speaker-elect and the formal acceptance of the election – 'a qui le Roy s'agrea bien' – either by the King himself, or his representative. At this point, and so it had become established in the Parliament Rolls from 1427, the Speaker, overcome with simulated modesty, entered a formal plea to be excused the honour of election because of his own inadequacy. 'Your Speaker', declared Christopher Yelverton in a belittling display in 1597, 'ought to be a man big and comely, stately and well-spoken; his voice great, his carriage majestical, his nature haughty, and his purse plentiful. But contrarily, the stature of my body is small, myself not so well spoken, my voice low, my carriage of the common fashion, my nature soft and bashful, my purse thin, light, and never plentiful.' Just as formally, in 1597 as on other occasions, the plea was rejected by the Crown.

It was then usual for the Speaker to ask that 'the proceedings of the Commons may receive the most favourable construction, and that whatever he should speak which might be taken in evil part, might be imputed to his ignorance and not unto the Commons'. This, the Speaker's Protestation, was the most important part of the election procedure, for it safeguarded the interests and the role of both Speaker and Commons and emphasized that the Speaker was subject to the Commons' control; he was the Commons' delegate, their mouthpiece, therefore he could only speak, or act, as they gave him authority, and, provided he always did that, then they, not he, were responsible for any consequences.

Acceptance by the Crown of the Speaker's Protestation was indispensable to the proper working of Parliament, and from 1394 this was always recorded. From 1437 onwards the Parliament Rolls also record the 'enactment' of the Protestation – a sort of mutual insurance policy, which confirmed the Speaker's position vis-à-vis the Commons, the Lords and the Crown.

When his election had been confirmed by the monarch the Speaker embarked upon his 'ornate oration', a classical pot-pourri on the theme of how best a commonwealth should be governed, and ending with a traditional petition for privileges for himself and the members of the Lower House. For himself he asked the right to correct any incorrect reports he might make during his period of office, and the right of access to the monarch; for the House he asked for freedom from arrest and freedom of speech. In his reply the Lord Keeper granted these requests, as he was bound to do, but as often as not he added a word of advice that the Commons should not abuse their freedom from arrest and should understand that freedom of speech was not the right to speak without restraint on any and every matter. This routine completed, the work of the session could begin.

Duties of the Speaker

The first complete account of the duties of the Speaker is contained in John Hooker's *Order and Usage howe to keepe a Parliament*, published in 1571. Here the overall task of the Speaker is described as being 'to direct and guyde that house in good order and to see that ordinances, usages, and customs of the house to be firmly kept and observed'. This he should do by keeping an attendance register, recording there the names of absentees, who unless they had received a licence from the Speaker and the House, stood to be penalized by the loss of their wages under the statute of 1515.

He should decide the order of speaking during a debate; he should rule against unseemly language, and if a member strayed from the point, or, in the Speaker's opinion, failed even to get it in sight, he should be told 'to come to his matter'. Members who misbehaved were open to his correction, and, if the House advised it, to his punishment. If the liberties of the House were infringed and a member arrested the Speaker was to punish whosoever was responsible, committing him to the custody of the Sergeant-at-Arms, or elsewhere. It was his responsibility to see that the proceedings of the House were recorded, and that arrangements were made for the custody of the *Journals*, begun unofficially in 1547, and for the safe-keeping of bills.

In dealing with private bills, or official bills, which in the late fifteenth and early sixteenth centuries had superseded Commons' petitions as the normal basis of legislation, the Speaker in theory acted differently from the Speaker in practice. According to Hooker, the Speaker would choose which bills were to be read and when, only if the House failed to do so; he read all bills and explained them to the House, and his function here was as stated in a formal ruling of the House in 1604: 'if any doubt arise upon a bill, the Speaker is to explain, but not sway the House with argument or dispute'. After its second reading he ordered a bill to be engrossed; after the third reading he put the question, appointed tellers if a division was called for, and himself only voted in case of a tie.

In all this it was the Speaker's duty to be impartial. His actions over bills, however, were not so aloof and impartial. In medieval times he made use of his position to further the progress of private bills, his goodwill in the matter being rewarded gratefully by the sponsors after the event, but sometimes in advance. In the reign of Elizabeth the success or failure of a private bill depended entirely upon the Speaker – indeed, the best definition of a 'private bill' is one that afforded parliamentary officials the opportunity for getting fees out of somebody.

Generally, however, public took priority over private bills, and there is no doubt that the Speaker and the Privy Councillors, who had their own committee to draw up the government's programme of legislation before the session began, worked closely together to ensure favourable notice in the House of such bills as the government was especially interested in; conversely, his delaying tactics could also be relied upon.

Ruthless objectivity would hardly have been at home in the Tudor period, and there were occasions when the Speaker's interest was too apparent, his furthering of a measure too blatant to escape censure in the Commons. 'In some such matters as he hath favoured, he hath without licence of this House spoken to the bill,' complained Anthony Cope, Puritan Member for Banbury in 1581 of the Speaker, Solicitor-General Popham, 'and in some other cases, which he did not favour and like of, he would prejudice the speeches of the members of this House with the question.'

Until the deepening of the rift between King and Parliament in Charles I's reign made the dual relationship intolerable, the Speaker felt no embarrassment as the servant of two masters, and both masters were generally well satisfied. Through him the opinions and wishes of the Commons could be made known;

and the monarch made full use of him, to pass on information
and instructions to the Commons, and, when necessary, to keep
them in order. When in 1532, after the publication of Thomas
Abell's book in support of Catherine of Aragon, *Invicta Veritas*,
a Member of Parliament moved that the House implore the King
to take Catherine back, thus avoiding the bastardizing of Mary
'and other great mischiefs', Henry sent for the Speaker, Sir
Thomas Audley, and instructed him to tell the Commons 'of
the King's marvelling that the House inter-meddled in a cause
not determinable there'.

The monarch could also keep an ear to the ground by having
the Speaker report on proceedings in the House, and we must
assume that the report was usually more informative and less
flippant than that of Speaker Sir John Popham, who, when asked
by Elizabeth 'What hath passed in the Commons' House?'
replied 'If it please your Majesty, seven weeks'.

Payment of the Speaker

When Sir Edward Seymour was elected Speaker in 1673 he was
the first for more than 150 years who was not a lawyer. No
doubt lawyers, as men of affairs, were considered by Crown and
Commons alike as best fitted to serve their interests in a businesslike way, but in monetary terms a lawyer found no profit in his
term as Speaker. Of all M.P.s the Speaker was the only one who
had to be present at all times during the parliamentary session;
he was, therefore, for that time unable to continue in active
legal practice. His loss by way of legal fees and expenses involved
in his office might amount to £2,000, which was the figure calculated by Sergeant Puckering, Speaker in the successive Parliaments of 1584–5 and 1586–7.

Under the Yorkists the Speaker would appear to have been
paid an honorarium, the amount varying according to the official
value placed on his services; but from 1485 at least, 'in considera-
cion of the laudable service to us done' a fee of £100 by Privy
Seal warrant 'at the Exchequer' was paid to the Speaker for each
session of Parliament, irrespective of its duration. The *King's*

Book of Payments records a further £100 paid to the Speaker in January 1513 and, although Sir Thomas More's term of office had not exactly turned out as expected, Wolsey wrote to the King in August 1523, recommending the double fee: 'it hath been accustomed that the Speakers of the parliaments, in consideration of their diligence and pains taken, have had, though the parliament hath been right soon finished, above the £100 ordinary, a reward of £100 for the better maintenance of their household and other charges sustained in the same'. There is, however, no evidence to suggest that 'double hire' continued to be paid; in fact, soon after this the single fee of £100 per session appears to have been established as the Speaker's reward.

In addition to this fee there were other 'perks' attached to the Speakership. John Hooker said the Speaker was entitled to a fee of £5 for every private bill which passed both Houses, while William Lambarde, writing in 1587, quoted the same fee payable just for every private bill, even before its first reading. At such a rate Sir John Neale has estimated that a Speaker in one of Elizabeth's later Parliaments, Christopher Yelverton, received between £200 and £300 from this source.

From the City of London a 'free gift' was made to the Speaker of every Elizabethan Parliament, almost as a retainer, 'for his lawful favour to be borne and showed in the Parliament House towards this city and their affairs there'; and the miscellaneous offerings – a present of fish from the Cinque Ports, a 'garnysshe large vessel' from the London Pewterers' Company – indicate clearly yet another strand in the web of patronage of which the Speaker was undoubtedly a part.

The Sergeant-at-Arms

Besides the Speaker there were only two other House of Commons officers in the pay of the Crown – the Sergeant-at-Arms and the Clerk. The Sergeant-at-Arms, who was an esquire or gentleman, was appointed for life 'to attend upon the Speaker ... At the special petition of the Commons in the Parliament at Leycester by letters patent' in 1415. He was the 'Royal Sergeant', specially attendant on the sovereign and was simply seconded to the Commons to act under the Speaker's instructions to preserve good order, and to enforce parliamentary privilege against those outside the House who constantly interfered with the M.P.s.

When the House was sitting the Sergeant-at-Arms was 'to be attendant upon the Speaker' and was to 'carry the mace before him'. He took up his position at the bar of the House, and, according to John Hooker, 'He ought to keep the inner door fast and to suffer none to come into the House during the time of sitting, unless he be one of the House, or come [with] message from the Higher House, or be willed by the House to come in'. He had a book containing the names of all members, so he knew whom he was to admit.

On a warrant from the Speaker he would apprehend anyone who had infringed the dignity or privileges of the House and commit them to whatever place of detention the House prescribed. From the time of Elizabeth onwards a frequent duty was to visit Westminster Hall to gather up lawyer members who were attending to their professional work, and to summon them to the House to attend to their parliamentary duties.

In the Commons the Sergeant-at-Arms was the counterpart of Black Rod in the House of Lords, and acted as messenger between the Commons and the Lords, carrying protests, resolutions, or petitions from the Lower House. He was besides 'Housekeeper', and in this capacity had to provide extensive services at Westminster, which involved the provision of supplies and the employment of servants.

By the letters patent of 1415 the Sergeant-at-Arms was to receive for 'service and attendance £10 a year of the issues of the City of London'; in the Tudor period his fee from the Crown amounted to £18 5 0 a year, based on a rate of 12d a day, besides a new livery every Christmas. He did not receive any additional reward at the end of a session, so he relied heavily on additional fees and tips, by which he probably made more than ten times his customary fee in the course of a year.

As with his master, the Speaker, his support in the passage of a private bill could be purchased, as could some appointments which came within his gift. From the culprit arrested by the Sergeant in his capacity as tipstaff and gaoler he collected 20/-, and 10/- a day while he remained in the sergeant's custody; from all members of the Commons he levied, on admittance to the House, a fee of 2/- each burgess and 2/6 each knight, which, by 1597, had become accepted as a customary charge. By that time too, the Sergeant and his helpers, who were not paid by the Crown, and who, therefore, lived out of the fees of their master, took a share of the levy which was made upon all M.P.s to provide for the relief of the poor.

The Clerk of the House

If it was the Sergeant-at-Arms' duty to uphold the dignity of the Commons, it was the function of the Clerk of the House to handle the essential mechanics of the parliamentary session. Next to the Speaker he was the most important of the Commons' officers, without whom nothing of any practical value could have been achieved.

When the Lords and Commons met as one body there may have been a Clerk and an Assistant Clerk serving Parliament; when they began meeting separately in the early fourteenth century it may be that the Clerk remained with the Lords, his assistant went with the Commons, for the style of the Commons' Clerk – 'Underclerk of the Parliaments attending upon the Commons' – lends support to this conclusion.

Much of the business of the early House of Commons was concerned with the presentation of petitions (private bills, as they became later), so the primary duty of the Clerk was to read them aloud to the House. Later he had to write out the bills for the first reading; after the second reading he would write on the back of the bill the names of the members of the Committee dealing with the next stage, and when and where the Committee was to meet; any amendments made at this stage the Clerk wrote in on the actual document itself, and then, finally, the bill was engrossed.

The Clerk was appointed by the Crown by letters patent, and

was paid a fee half-yearly by the Crown, and a reward besides at
the end of the session. Under Henry VIII and Mary the Clerk
received a fee of £5 a year, but under Edward VI and Elizabeth
this was raised to £10 (the Clerk of the Upper House received at
this time £40 a year). The larger part of the Clerk's income, however, came from gratuities from M.P.s, which might be a few
shillings from each at the end of a Parliament, and from various
fees payable for certain of his, and his staff's services.

He received a fee from all private bills, for rewriting bills and
for engrossing them on parchment when they reached the third
reading; for providing a copy of a bill to a member, or any other
interested party, the Clerk charged at a rate of so much per line
for a paper copy, or so much per 'press', or sheet of parchment.

The issue of a licence to a member to depart before the end of a
parliamentary session was entered into the *Journal* on the payment of a fee, as were the details of cases of offences against the
House or its members. And, inevitably, many other opportunities
of a more unofficial, but no less customary kind, were afforded
the Clerk to augment his income: the City of London, for example,
made him a fairly regular payment, as it did to the Speaker and
the Sergeant-at-Arms, in gratitude, not only for what they had
received, but in anticipation of benefits that were yet to come.

Undoubtedly, the Clerk, sitting behind the table of the House,
which was no more than 'a little board before him to write and
lay his books upon', was a man of considerable influence and
prestige. Much of his status he acquired during the Tudor period,
for then, although he remained a servant of the Crown, he nevertheless became more and more committed to the interests of the
Commons and much more professional in his approach to his
parliamentary duties.

Two distinguished Clerks, who between them spanned the
period from 1547 to 1602, were John Seymour and Fulk Onslow.
John Seymour, Member for Great Bedwin in Wiltshire in Henry
VIII's last Parliament of 1545, was appointed Clerk in 1548
(although he appears to have started the job in Edward VI's
first Parliament in 1547) and held the office until his death in
1567. During this time Seymour, for his own interest, kept a day-

to-day diary, just rough notes, of proceedings in the House of Commons. It began just as a record of petitions – when they were presented and how they fared – but gradually he extended its scope to include notes on such things as the attendance of members, rulings of the House in matters affecting privilege, and, from 1553, a record of all divisions in the House. Such a record was really essential for a Clerk approaching his duties in a businesslike way, but its value to the House became apparent in 1581 when, the Speakership falling vacant, recourse was made to Seymour's diary, 'the original book of notes', to check on the matter of procedure in this case.

Fulk Onslow continued the journal, but with some significant improvements. Seymour's rough notes were roughly jotted down but Onslow, after parliamentary hours, wrote up a fair copy of his rough notes in more legible handwriting and on a folio sheet instead of the smaller quarto page used by Seymour.

However, when Onslow began including précis of speeches made in the House he was establishing a rather dangerous precedent. To have kept this up would have demanded too much of an already quite busy enough Clerk, and the danger was in having in black-and-white what members had actually said within the House. Charles I, in fact, did demand to see the *Journal of the House* as the Clerk's journal became in 1623, to check on what a particular member had said; and because this could obviously happen again the House promptly resolved in 1628 that 'the entry of the clerk of particular men's speeches was without warrant at all times'.

This ruling, however, did not detract from the inestimable value of the *Journal* as an official record of proceedings in the House. In 1623 a Committee was appointed 'to survey the Clerk's Book of Entries every Saturday in the afternoon', and from then on the maintenance of the *Journal* was one of the Under Clerk to the Parliament's most important duties.

Unfortunately, although the Clerk of the House of Lords was able to store records and documents in the Stone Tower in Old Palace Yard his counterpart in the Lower House had no such official depository, and had to keep all his papers – copies of bills,

journals, and so on – at his own home, which was not very satisfactory because so very insecure. In the latter part of the seventeenth century, however, space was found for the Commons'
records, but ironically, the fire that destroyed the Palace of
Westminster in 1834 destroyed them all – with the exception of
the *Journals*.

[6] PROCEDURE

Commons' meeting place

From 1332, when Lords and Commons met separately, the
Commons rarely sat elsewhere than in the Chapel and Refectory
of Westminster Abbey. But in 1547 St Stephen's Chapel in the
middle of the Royal Palace of Westminster, which already housed
the courts of justice and the administrative departments of
government, was made over to the Crown by the Chantries Act,
and the upper part was 'assigned for the house of parliament' on
loan from the Crown. St Stephen's Chapel remained the Commons' permanent home until 1834 when it was destroyed by fire.

Accommodation

John Hooker, M.P. for Exeter, described the internal arrangements of the House of Commons Chamber in 1571; 'This House is
framed and made like unto a theatre, being four rows of seats
one above another, round about the House. [These were bench
seats, backs being added during the Commonwealth.] At the
higher end, in the middle of the lowest row, is a seat made for the
Speaker, where he is appointed to sit; and before him sitteth the
Clerk of the House, having a little board before him to write and
lay his books upon. Upon the lower row, next to the Speaker, sit
all such of the Queen's Privy Council and head officers as be
knights or burgesses for that House; but after, everyone sitteth

as he cometh, no difference being there held of any degree, because each man in that place is of like calling, saving that the knights and burgesses for London and York do sit on the right side, next to the Councillors.' There was no door into the Chamber at the east end, that is behind the Speaker, so the cross-benches came right up to his chair on either side, which meant that the Speaker could be primed, and his guidance of the business of the House regulated, by whispered instructions from the royal officials and Privy Councillors sitting at his elbows.

There was, at the west end, a vestibule, or 'outer room', under the jurisdiction of the Sergeant-at-Arms and his assistants, in which, according to Hooker, 'the under clerks do sit, as also such as be suitors and attendant to that House; and whensoever the House is divided upon any bill, then the room is voided'.

Over this vestibule, or 'lobby' as it came to be called, the House had its own Committee Room, but this was only used in an emergency – if urgent consideration had to be given to a bill, or if it was necessary to hold a meeting early in the morning before the House had assembled. Generally Committees were held in the place most immediately convenient to the Committee members themselves, the Inns of Court very often, the Guildhall or the Temple Church, or, if Privy Councillors were members of the Committee, it might meet in the Exchequer or the Star Chamber, perhaps even in the chambers of Mr Treasurer, or Mr Secretary himself.

Seating accommodation for members in the Commons' Chamber was adequate when the Commons first used St Stephen's Chapel, but then there were only just over 300 members; by the beginning of the seventeenth century their number had increased to almost 500 and then there just were not seats for everyone. A resolution of the House in 1604 pointed out that as members were turning up 'in greater multitudes than heretofore had been usual' they 'do want convenient room to sit in the place accustomed for their meeting; and by reason of this lack of room, many were forced to stand in the entrance and midst of the House, contrary to order'. Substantial structural alterations

were obviously necessary to solve the problem, so the House
'required . . . that the officers of His Majesty's works do immediately give order for erecting and fitting such and so many rooms
and seats as the whole House may sit, and attend the service
with more ease and conveniency'. These required alterations,
however, were not carried out, and the House continued to suffer
(as, indeed, it still does) from the disadvantages of a Chamber in
which all the members cannot be accommodated at one and the
same time.

Hours of sitting

Contrary to our present practice, in the early Tudor period the
Commons sat each day, except Sunday, from 8 a.m. to 11 a.m.,
the times coinciding with those observed by the law courts. An
attempt by the Speaker in 1571 to open a sitting with prayers at
8.30 a.m. so that members had more time to be in their places
did not work out at all satisfactorily; so much time was lost, in
fact, that within only a few days the House was voting to meet at
7 a.m. to make up for it. In general, however, proceedings began
at 8 a.m., with the occasional Committee meeting an hour or two
earlier. The day's sitting usually ended at about noon, although
there was no hard and fast rule about this. Sometimes business
would go on until nearer 1 p.m., or, latest of all, to beyond 3 in
the afternoon, which is what happened in 1593, when a bill
against sectaries was being debated at the Report Stage. On that
occasion hunger eventually got the better of religious suscepti-
bilities, and, having sat for so long behind closed doors 'we were
content' wrote one member, 'to yield to anything, so we might
rise. I assure you, Sir, a great many of us caught such a faintness
there, with so long fasting, having neither meat in our bellies nor
wit in our heads, that we shall not, I doubt me, be able to make
a wise speech there while we live.'

Some afternoon sessions became necessary to deal with increasing pressure on parliamentary time, but they were no more
successful than the modern expedient of meeting occasionally in
the morning. Members serving on Committees could not attend

T.P.—6

in the House, and many members spent their afternoons engaged about their own affairs and were not prepared to do otherwise.

There were a few afternoon sittings, however, in the reigns of Edward VI and Mary; in 1563 the Commons met on 21 afternoons, and in 1571 it was decided to meet for two hours on Monday, Wednesday and Friday afternoons, then from 3 p.m. to 5 p.m. on every afternoon to deal with first and second readings of private bills. There were more extended sittings in 1572 and 1575, but then the practical difficulties were accepted as being too great, until in Elizabeth's last Parliament Cecil reintroduced them so that the session itself could be curtailed as he believed 'we consume our time now in unnecessary disputation'.

Secrecy and strangers

In theory at least, parliamentary proceedings were secret. Privy Councillors did take an oath of secrecy, but Parliament matters, especially at times of particular conflict and, therefore, interest, must have become fairly widely known by what we should nowadays called 'inspired leaks' as garrulous or vain members moved about the inns and eating houses of London. Sir Robert Cecil, at the height of the monopolies struggle in Parliament, may have professed himself shocked because 'Parliamentary matters are ordinarily talked of in the streets. I have heard myself, being in my coach, these words spoken aloud: "God prosper those that further the overthrow of these monopolies. God send the prerogative touch not our liberty." ' – but from his experience he can hardly have been surprised.

Should anyone not a member of the House attend its meetings the dignity of the Commons was aroused, its authority was defended by the Sergeant-at-Arms, and action was swift and thorough. Richard Robinson, a skinner by trade, was found in 1584 to have been in the House 'for the space of two hours, during the whole time of the speeches delivered by Mr Chancellor and the Vice-Chamberlain', and 'being no member of the House', he was brought to the bar of the House, 'stript to the shirt, and his pockets searched, and then remanded to the custody of the

Sergeant-at-Arms'. The Commons were taking no chances, and after a committee had investigated his career and character he was again brought to the bar of the House, censured by the Speaker, and, having sworn to divulge nothing of what he had seen or heard, was made to take the Oath of Supremacy – just to be sure that he was not in the pay of Rome.

The chandler and butcher who had 'presumed to come into the House' through 'ignorance and meer simplicity' were similarly treated in 1586 'and afterwards departed'. Nor are these just isolated examples. Others during the Tudor and Stuart periods were treated to 'a grave admonition' from the Speaker, fined (the fine paid to the Sergeant-at-Arms), and 'sworn before they departed to keep secret what they had heard there'.

Parliamentary oaths

Members of the House of Commons had been one of the several classes of people who had not been required to take the Oath of Supremacy as laid down in the 1559 Act, which had meant that members could be chosen without the application of a religious test to their suitability or dependability. This wide range of choice was, however, curtailed when the 'Act for the Assurance of the Queen's Power' (a forerunner of penal legislation against the Roman Catholics) was passed in 1563; for its purpose was 'to abolish the Pope's usurped supremacy and prevent his and his instrument's traitorous attempts against the Queen's person, crown, and kingdom; discover persons popishly affected; and seclude them from sitting or voting in the Commons House'. Although there were several Roman Catholic peers the loyalty of the members of the House of Lords was not in question, and no excluding oath was required of them until 1678.

The oath, which was not administered until 1566, required every M.P., before he took his seat, to declare, before the Lord Steward or his deputy, that the Queen was 'the only supreme governor' in spiritual and temporal matters, 'and that no foreign prince, person, prelate, state or potentate hath or ought to have any jurisdiction, power, superiority, pre-eminence or authority, ecclesiastical or spiritual within this realm'. Failure to take the oath meant that a man was disabled from becoming a member of Parliament, and made him subject to 'such pains and penalties as if he had presumed to sit in the House without election, return, or authority'.

In an intolerant age it would be unreasonable to expect Parliament, which had so revelled in its participation in the break with Rome, to have been up in arms over the harsh requirement of the Oath of Supremacy; nevertheless, there was some opposition expressed in both Houses.

Lord Montagu took an enlightened and practical view, attacking the unnecessary discrimination against a harmless minority 'forasmuch as the Catholics of this realm disturb not, nor hinder the public affairs of the realm, neither spiritual nor temporal. They dispute not; they preach not; they disobey not the Queen; they cause no trouble nor tumults among the people; so that no man can say that thereby the realm doth receive any hurt nor damage by them. ... And where there is no sore nor grief, medecines are superfluous and also hurtful and dangerous.'

When it appeared that the Catholics were determined both to hurt and damage the realm the penal legislation was either more strictly enforced, or increased. An Act of 1610 required M.P.s to take the Oath of Allegiance and Abjuration, which had been called for in 1606 after the panic of the Gunpowder Plot from all over the age of eighteen, or any nobleman or woman suspected of being a Papist. Four years later the House still felt there were 'Papists among us', and so ordered 'that every member of the Commons shall take the sacrament at St Margaret's Church'.

The practice of members attending to hear a sermon at Westminster Abbey at the opening of a new Parliament began in 1563 and continued into the seventeenth century. After the service the members returned to 'the great room called the Court of Whitehall, or the Court of Request', where the Oath of Supremacy, required by the Act of 1563, was administered by the Lord Steward of the Royal Household, or his deputy; after this the Commons proceeded to their own chamber to elect their Speaker.

Daily prayers

Daily prayers in the House seem also to date from this time, and the first actual record of this is contained in the Resolution of 1571, which directed that 'the litany shall be read every day as in the last Parliament, and also a prayer said by Mr Speaker as he shall think fittest for this time, to be begun every day at half-past eight a.m., and that each then making default shall forfeit for every time fourpence to the poor man's box'. It was part of the Clerk's duties to read the Litany, at least until 1597, when a minister was appointed to read the prayers, receiving for his services a payment of £10, which was taken from the collection made for the poor.

As the period progressed a greater solemnity marked the Speaker's prayer, and his intercession in the first Parliament of James I's reign is of particular interest in the light of the parliamentary struggle that was about to begin:

Oh God most great and glorious, which dwelleth in the Heavens over all, yet humbleth thyself to behold the things that are done upon the earth, We, thy people and the sheep of thy pasture, assembled by thy providence to the performance of this high service whereupon the honour of thy Name, the beauty of thy Church among us, the glory of our King and the wealth of our State doth depend, Let the good of this whole island move our care and zeal, which consisting in the safety and honour of the King and the enacting and execution of good laws, let us be wisely careful and faithfully zealous for the person of our King, whom thou, the King of Kings, hath in mercy set over us. And because no law can be good that is not agreeable to thy law, which containeth the fundamental equity of our laws; in making laws to govern thy people, let us always have an eye to thy law, not digressing from the holy equity thereof; and what through thy mercy we shall here profitably enact, we pray thee through the whole Kingdom it may be truly executed, that our great labour may not be disgraced with little fruit.

Conduct of Members of the House

This solemnity was the result of a greater activity and growing
confidence on the part of the Commons; and so too were their
Orders, those rules for maintaining the decorum of the House
and for the proper conduct of members during debate, and during
the whole of their attendance at Westminster. The Elizabethan
period was an especially important one for the development of
these rules, and the Speaker, of course, was especially important for seeing that they were properly carried out.

Hats were worn inside the House; boots and rapiers were
allowed, too, but spurs were not – 'by ancient order'. A member
wishing to speak rose, removed his hat and began, unless others
were also on their feet at the same time, and then the Speaker
decided the speaking order, making his choice in accordance
with Sir Edward Coke's decision of 1593 that 'the party who
speaks against the last speaker is to be heard first'.

Members addressed their speeches to the Speaker and were
expected to 'use reverent and discreet speeches, to leave curios-
ties of form, to speak to the matter . . . and not to spend too
much time in unnecessary motions or superfluous arguments' –
invaluable advice both then and now! Such stipulations must,
however, have been given a pretty wide and tolerant interpretation, or Francis Bacon would surely never have been allowed
to get away with this:

I, Mr Speaker have a bill here, which I know I shall be no sooner ready
to offer, but you will be as ready to receive and approve. I liken this
bill to that sentence of the poet, who set this as a paradox in the fore-
front of his book, 'First water, then gold'; preferring necessity before
pleasure. . . . This, Mr Speaker, is no bill of state, nor of novelty, like
a stately gallery for pleasure but neither to dine in or sleep in; but this
bill is a bill of repose, of quiet, of profit, and of true and just dealing;
the title whereof is 'An act for the better suppressing of abuses in
weights and measures'.

One can imagine that much time was taken up with lengthy
set speeches, carefully prepared and written down, bristling with
biblical and classical allusions yet of a quality to hold the House's

attention. However, Sir Thomas Smith in *The Commonwealth of England*, 'the most important description of the constitution and government of England written in the Tudor Age' (*DNB*) and published in 1581, says that a member was only permitted to speak once on one bill on any one day, 'for else one or two with altercation would spend all the time', so one can understand than when a member rose to speak he certainly made the most of it.

But if the House listened in silence, as was customary, to long but eloquent and meaty orations, they had little patience with those which were poorly phrased, tedious, or excessively partisan, and such a performance was punctuated (or, on occasion, abbreviated) by laughter, coughing and murmuring. 'After this speech', D'Ewes noted in 1601, 'an old doctor of civil law spake, but because he was too long and spake too low, the House hawked and spat, and kept a great coil to make him an end.' For some unaccountable reason hissing was classed as disorderly conduct, but 'hawking and spitting' were not!

The Commons' *Journals* contain frequent references, particularly in the first of the Parliaments of James I, to the adoption of resolutions by the House to give the Speaker greater power in dealing with irrelevance. It was 'Agreed that if any superflous motion or tedious speech be offered in the House, the party is to be directed and ordered by the Speaker', and 'If any man speaks impertinently or besides the question in hand, it stands within the orders of the House for Mr Speaker to interrupt him, and to know the pleasure of the House, whether they will hear him further'.

Impertinence in speaking to, or about, his colleagues in the House was also frowned upon, and its restriction likewise became the province of the Speaker. No member was to be referred to by name 'but only by circumlocution'; and 'no reviling or nipping words must be used', although the increasing number of occasions during this period when parliamentary tempers were thoroughly roused caused this injunction to be often forgotten; as it was by the Elizabethan member in 1585, who, in replying to an attack made on his speech on the illegitimacy clause of the vagabonds bill, pointed out to his critic, somewhat indelicately, that 'there have been better bastards, are, and will be than ever he was!' Here was a certain case for the Speaker, and there is no doubt that this part of his job became more difficult as the period progressed.

The day's business over, lapses like this were set aside and decorum returned, for it was required by their own motion of 1581 'that Mr Speaker and the residue of the House of the better sort of calling would always, at the raising of the House, depart and go forth in comely and civil sort for the reverence of the House, in turning about with a low curtsy, like as they do make at their coming into the House; and not so unseemly and rudely to thrust and throng out as of late time hath been disorderly used'.

Legislation

Before the Tudor period, because petitions formed the basis of all legislation, Parliament was a law-declaring, rather than a law-making assembly, but from the reign of Henry VII enactment by bills for all kinds of legislation replaced the petitions. This began with the King drawing up laws – government measures, we could call them – which were put before the two Houses, whose agreement followed automatically. This procedure for public measures was then adapted for private petitions, and money grants, which, since Richard II's reign the Commons had been making to the Crown 'with the advice and assent' of the House of Lords, were presented in the form of bills.

Public bills were generally a source of parliamentary uneasiness, because lawyer members of the House of Commons had often acted in a professional capacity to draw them up, and for this they had taken fees; now although this was 'held to be lawful, yet cannot be but very convenient, seeing afterwards they are to be judges in the same case'. But if the writer of this early Stuart tract saw this 'foot-in-both-camps' situation as a mere inconvenience, Arthur Hall, Member for Grantham, in his pamphlet *Account of a Quarrel*, published in 1581, saw it rather as an example of sheer graft: 'to have clients in matters of parliament', he railed, 'is token of too much vility . . . What should I write of this most filthy, unnatural, and servile vice, which shall for a few angels make you plead as partially in parliament as in any other court, not regarding your country but the jinks in your pocket?' The cap undoubtedly fitted, and for this attack Hall was expelled from the House.

A private bill's sponsors pushed hard and in all possible ways to see that it got through, not least that inveterate puller of strings, the City of London, which besides making regular payments to the Speaker, Sergeant-at-Arms and Clerk, as we have seen, just as regularly set aside in their accounts another sum 'to further their interests' in some other ways. Sponsors sometimes provided dinner for members of a committee as an inducement to them to turn out in force to consider a particular private bill; they might, as the clothiers did in 1576, send out their own three-line whip for the same purpose. The simple fact of the matter is that the average M.P. had not the slightest aversion to any number of 'jinks' in his pocket – and the sponsors knew it.

Procedure on a bill

In the early Tudor period it was the House of Lords which did most of the legislative work as most bills were introduced there first. These roles were reversed in Elizabeth's reign, and then the Lords had time on their hands, not infrequently sending down to the now more busy and loquacious Lower House to ask if there were any bills ready to be passed up to them.

Such a change necessitated a tightening up of procedure in the Commons to deal with the increased amount of business, which could, and increasingly did, lead to congestion. The first reading of a bill tended to become simply a formality, although discussion was not ruled out; in fact, discussion did, occasionally take place, and an instance is recorded in 1601 of a bill actually being rejected at this stage.

A second and most significant change in procedure in the Commons was the increasing use of committees, for in committing a bill (and virtually every bill was committed) not only was an opportunity provided for making amendments in principle, or detail, but time was also saved by transferring debate from the floor of the House where lengthy oratory might well bog it down.

Committees, which were usually made up of members who had spoken to the bill on its second reading and had proposed amendments, were small, ranging in membership from 6 to 10 under Henry VIII and Edward VI, and from 10 to 20 in Elizabeth's early years. In the latter part of Elizabeth's reign, however, numbers increased; a committee of 1593 was made up of 60 members, besides all the Privy Councillors and the Sergeants-at-Law.

And the growth continued, at times the number of named committee members being joined by other members who were especially interested and could take part in the discussions, but could not vote. Large committees, therefore, became established as part of regular parliamentary practice, and by 1621 'few matters are debated in the House, but are referred to a committee and there debated. So either we must order ourselves to the old course of debating matters before we correct them; or else there is reason for more committees.'

From 1593 the Commons began to hold large committee meetings in the House itself, and this was the beginning of the instrument of procedure known as the 'Committee of the Whole House.' This was also a significant development, particularly in early Stuart times when relations between the Crown and Parliament were so tense, because on such occasions the Speaker, who was, after all, a royal servant, did not preside but 'a member by the consent of the whole House sat in the chair, as clerk to register the order of this committee; and by consent also was licensed to put on his hat'. 'It was the way that led most to truth. It was the more open way', insisted Sir John Eliot in 1628 when urging the House to consider the Petition of Right. 'It admitted of every man showing his reason and making answer upon the hearing of the reasons and arguments of other men.' It should be noted, however, that on these occasions the Speaker could still exercise his vote as a private member.

The general pattern of procedure on bills had, therefore, been established by the late sixteenth century and has remained the same ever since. From 1581 three readings of a bill was the accepted norm in both Houses, instead of the four, five, six, or even eight readings sometimes given during the reigns of Henry VIII, Edward VI and Mary. For the First Reading the Clerk read out the whole text of the bill, which might take anything up to two hours. After that, if he wished, a member could buy a copy of the bill from the Clerk, or read the actual bill in the Clerk's presence, which meant that the Second Reading would be accompanied by informed debate. Then the bill went to Committee, where formerly it could have been committed at any time, and amendments agreed by the majority were made. In reporting back to the House a member of the committee explained what amendments had been made, and the Clerk read out each amendment twice – sometimes just a single word which had been altered – so that the amendments, like the original bill, could be said to have received two readings. Debate followed, and it was then up to the Speaker to put the question that the bill be engrossed, that is that the final agreed text should be written out on parchment and from that the Third Reading would be made to the House.

When time pressed at the end of a session all stages of a bill might be raced through in a single morning, but this was exceptional. On the other hand prolonged discussion, like the eighteen speeches made to a bill at just one reading in 1572, was also unusual; the average was seven or eight speeches, and only on rare occasions did discussion of a single bill occupy two consecutive sittings.

Divisions

The Speaker put the question to the House orally, and the House voted orally, those in favour saying 'Yea', those against 'No'. If the Speaker could not distinguish the majority vote (and this was rare before 1558) a division – a procedure fully recognized by the Commons by 1554 – was taken. This was the procedure:

the Speaker appointed two members from each side to act as tellers, and then the 'Yeas', if they were the innovators, went out of the Chamber into the lobby, now vacated by the Sergeant and his officials and suitors. The 'Noes' remained seated and were counted where they sat, while the 'Yeas' were counted as they returned from the lobby. Then the tellers reported their count and the result was declared by the Speaker.

In a division the advantage clearly lay with those who stayed in the Chamber because 'though they that say Yea are most, yet many times when the House cometh to be divided, they are not found to be so, because many of them sit still, as loth to lose their places, and sometimes because they will not be observed to have said Yea; so the division of them is a disadvantage to the side that goeth out.' The government naturally exploited this reluctance. Speaker Yelverton put the question three times in 1593 and allowed a division, even though the 'Noes' were clearly in the majority, as they were again when the division was taken; indeed, only six of the seventeen divisions taken in the 1601 Parliament were won by the 'Yeas' – by those who left the Chamber, that is.

There is also evidence that a member might be forcibly restrained from getting up and voting for the 'Yeas', or conversely, might be energetically hauled to his feet to prevent his voting for the 'Noes'. The House seems to have regarded this as all part of the game, for, as Sir Walter Raleigh expressed it when a vote of 106 to 105 caused something of a rumpus in 1601, 'it is a small matter to pull one by the sleeve, for so I have done myself often times'.

After a division and a bill was passed it was normal procedure in 1571 'according to the ancient orders of this House in such cases', for it to be carried out and brought in again by Mr Vice-Chamberlain with the bill in his hand, followed and attended on by all the members of this House, then present, as well those that had just before given their voices against the passing . . . as those . . . with the passing'. But as the number of divisions steadily increased as the Tudor period progressed – there were seventeen in 1601, and only twenty-five in seven sessions from 1559 to 1581

– time did not permit of this processional ritual being preserved and it was gradually allowed to fall into disuse.

The Royal Assent

The final act of the parliamentary session was the giving of the Royal Assent to all the bills that had been passed by the two Houses. Their titles were read out by the Clerk of the Crown and the royal answer formula was spoken by the Clerk of the Parliaments. In public bills the form of assent was: 'Le Roi (La Reyne) le veult'; for private bills 'Soit faict comme il est désiré'. Acceptance of lay and clerical subsidies was made with the words 'Le Roi (La Reyne) remercie ses loyaulx subjects, accepte leur benevolence, et aussi le veult'.

Last of all came the Act of Pardon, when, the monarch standing, the Clerk tendered the thanks of the Commons, concluding 'et prient à Dieu qu'il vous donne, en santé, bonne vie et longue', to which the Commons, loyally, if at times a trifle reservedly, 'gave a loud Amen'.

Further Reading

Sir Goronwy Edwards, 'The Emergence of Majority Rule in the Procedure of the House of Commons', *Transactions of the Royal Historical Society*, 5th Series, Vol. 15 (1965).

G. R. Elton, *The Tudor Constitution*. Cambridge University Press (London, 1962).

J. P. Kenyon, *The Stuart Constitution*. Cambridge University Press (London, 1966).

*J. E. Neale, *The Elizabethan House of Commons*. Jonathan Cape (London, 1949).

*J. E. Neale, 'The Elizabethan Political Scene', in *Essays in Elizabethan History*. Jonathan Cape (London, 1958).

Wallace Notestein, *The English People on the Eve of Colonization, 1603–1630*. Harper & Brothers (New York, 1954).

A. F. Pollard, 'The Reformation Parliament as a Matrimonial Agency and its National Effects', *History*, Vol. XXI, No. 83 (December, 1936).

*E. & A. G. PORRITT, *The Unreformed House of Commons*, Vol. I, England and Wales. Cambridge University Press (London, 1903).

*J. S. ROSKELL, *The Commons and their Speakers in English Parliaments, 1376–1523*. Manchester University Press (Manchester, 1965).

*J. R. TANNER, *Tudor Constitutional Documents*. Cambridge University Press (London, 1922).

* These books provide the basis for what has been written here on 'The Mechanics of Parliament'.

PART III
Crown versus Parliament – The Growth of Opposition

[7] FROM 1485 TO 1529

Henry VII (1485–1509)

The distinctive Crown–Parliament relationship of the Tudor period did not begin with Henry VII. He generally paid little attention to Parliament and required little of it. His attitude, in fact, was not so very different from that of his Yorkist predecessors; like them he made sure that his own financial resources were cultivated and augmented, so that parliamentary grants would never become a matter of absolute necessity, and even when they were required to support his quasi-warlike purposes he saw to it that his actual expenditure was considerably less than the grants he received.

The situation, therefore, was one that required that only a few Parliaments should meet – only seven met in the twenty-four years of his reign, their sessions totalling just ten and a half months – but Henry could not dispense with them altogether. To begin with, parliamentary assent was needed for legislation. Here Henry was able to dominate proceedings in Parliament by turning to his own advantage a precedent set by Richard III in the only Parliament he called in 1484; official bills in increasing numbers were introduced into Parliament and enacted as statutes. What had been an innovation under Richard III became firmly established procedure under Henry VII and, although bills were still introduced on the Commons' initiative, these government bills were not only more numerous, but also more important.

In this way Henry VII crowded into the statute books a whole series of measures – correcting abuses, remedying grievances, amending the law and implementing various elements of economic policy, as well as confirming and strengthening by statute previous enactments. The example set by Henry as a legislator by parliamentary statute was clearly followed by his son and, in particular, by Thomas Cromwell.

Then again, to Henry VII, as to the Yorkist kings Edward IV and Richard III, Parliament was essential to record the validity of his royal title; that is not to say that Henry VII had any intention of allowing Parliament to make him King, for, as he pointed out 'with his own mouth' in his first Parliament, which met on 7 November 1485, 'his coming to the Right and Crown of England' was 'as much by just Title of inheritance as by the true judgment of God in granting to him Victory over his enemy in the Field'.

Thirdly, as has been mentioned already, extraordinary taxation required parliamentary consent, and as the nobility and gentry (unlike their compeers in most other parts of Europe) were liable for direct taxation, their influence was on the side of Parliament as a means whereby their own, as well as the interests of others, could be safeguarded. Infrequent Parliaments, therefore, meant infrequent taxation, so the fact that only one Parliament met in the last twelve years of Henry's reign was a source of all-round satisfaction, not least to the King, because it testified to the continuing success of his own careful and ubiquitous financial policies.

Henry's relations with Parliament were realistically competent, and, for the most part at least, eminently satisfactory. After a first session of less than five weeks, Henry's first Parliament in 1485 had, by an Act of Resumption, restored Crown lands, which had been alienated since the beginning of the Wars of the Roses in 1455, and had granted the King (as it had Richard III) tunnage and poundage and the wool subsidies for life;

further, Lords and Commons had joined in a prayer to the King that he should marry Elizabeth, the 'White Rose of York'.

The united aim of King and people was to remove the shadow of civil strife, and to put England on her feet, economically and politically, within the European framework. Measures designed to preserve public order were put in hand in Henry's second Parliament, which assembled on 9 November 1487, and lasted for five weeks, and in granting two-tenths and two-fifteenths Parliament consented to the first direct taxation of the reign.

This first enthusiasm, however, was not always reflected in the country as a whole, nor sustained in Parliament. The third Parliament – the longest of the reign – which met in three sessions of six, seven and five weeks between 13 January 1489 and the end of February 1490, ran into trouble in voting £75,000 in February 1489, to maintain an army of 10,000 men. Previous taxes allowed by Parliament had aroused unrest, including a rising in North Yorkshire, and of this further grant no more than a third had been collected a year later, and one-tenth and one-fifteenth were all that the Commons were prepared to offer to make up the difference.

Further royal demands were made in Henry's fourth Parliament (17 October 1491 – 5 March 1492) as the intervention in the affairs of Brittany was not going at all well, and money, which had been raised by a 'benevolence', had not come up to expectations. The Speaker in this Parliament was Richard Empson of Easton Neston, near Towcester, M.P. for Northamptonshire and Attorney-General for the Duchy of Lancaster, so Henry's demands in Parliament would certainly be pushed to the hilt. Within three weeks the Commons had voted two-tenths and two-fifteenths, and had promised that a third subsidy would also be granted if the King should campaign abroad for longer than eight months – evidence of Parliament's support for Henry's policy certainly, but an indication of the Speaker's influence in such matters, too.

The emergency created by the presence in Scotland of the Flemish pretender, Perkin Warbeck, and his recognition by James IV, accounted for the summoning of his fifth Parliament by Henry on 14 October 1495, to prepare against a possible rebellion. The Speaker was Robert Drury, Knight of the Shire for Suffolk, and probably deputy-Chief Steward of the Duchy of Lancaster estates south of the river Trent, who, like Empson, stood high in Court favour. Absolution from the penalties of treason was offered to potential supporters of a second Yorkist rising by the Act 'for security under the King *de facto*', and although no regular subsidy was voted parliamentary authority was given to a recently issued proclamation, which had threatened with imprisonment any who neglected within the space of three months to contribute to a recently granted benevolence.

Henry's survival in 1497 was assured by the continuing success of his policies at home and abroad. In the Magnus Intercursus Archduke Philip had agreed to the expulsion of Yorkist troublemakers from the Netherlands, a new treaty for the marriage of his daughter to Henry's elder son, Arthur, had been made with Ferdinand of Spain, and an abortive Scottish attack served to diminish James IV's enthusiasm for the 'Duke of York'; it also served Henry with an excuse to raise some more money. He attempted to anticipate an undertaking given by a Great Council of the Lords and 'certain Burgesses and Merchants' that his next Parliament would grant him £120,000, by raising loans, but only to about half that amount.

His sixth Parliament (16 January–13 March 1497) voted two-tenths and two-fifteenths to bridge the gap, happy that the matter of fund-raising was being dealt with in a proper constitutional way. Nevertheless, however benign the attitude of Parliament, the additional taxation precipitated the Cornish Rising of 1497, its leaders Michael Joseph and Thomas Flamank, objecting to the payment of taxes for 'a smal commocion made of ye Scottes, which was asswaged and ended in a moment'. The rising was quelled, but it might have suggested to Henry that Parliament might well be given a rest for a while, and anyway the success of his economic and financial policies had made him, by this time (and provided no totally unforeseen expenditure became necessary), quite independent of parliamentary grants.

But Henry VII, in his early years not mean but extremely

careful, had, in his later years a great fascination for money for
its own sake, together with a variety of dubious ways of amassing
it. In his last Parliament in 1504 he demanded the grant of three-
fifteenths (c. £90,000) as feudal 'aids' on the occasion of the
marriage of his daughter, Margaret, and the posthumous knighting
of his son, Arthur. Parliament would have none of it, in particular the young Thomas More, one of its burgesses, who made
'such arguments and reasons against, that the King's demands
thereby were clean overthrown'; as one of Henry's Privy Councillors reported to him, 'a beardless boy had disappointed all his
purpose'.

Henry had to be satisfied with the £30,000 he accepted to
mollify the Commons. Not that he needed the money; therefore, he did not need Parliament. An Act of this same year
authorizing Henry to repeal attainders illustrates this independence, and although he justified such a measure on the grounds
that he did not propose 'without grete necessarye and urgent
causes, of long tyme to calle and summone a newe Parliament',
the resolution may well have been more a matter of personal convenience than out of consideration 'for the eas of his Subgiects'.

It was six years before Parliament met again, in the second
year of the reign of his son. By that time, so many believed, a
new age had dawned; the shrewd industry and cool resolution of
Henry VII held none of the glitter and romance of the precocious
Renaissance prince who succeeded him at the age of seventeen
on 22 April 1509.

Henry VIII (1509-29)

Henry VIII, though lacking in experience, lacked nothing in his
determination to please and impress. Within a year of his accession, when the festivities accompanying his coronation and
marriage were over, he met his first Parliament (21 January–
23 February 1510).

The King, for his part, intended to follow a more equitable
and humane fiscal policy, free from the taint of his father's last
years, and, as a sign of gratitude and loyalty, the Commons

voted him the wool subsidies and tunnage and poundage for life, with the additional grant of two-tenths and two-fifteenths. An extravagant young King like Henry was bound, sooner or later, to see a lot of Parliament, but his resolution in early days was to summon it for regular meetings, and Chancellor Thomas Warham, Archbishop of Canterbury, spoke of this necessity in Henry's second Parliament, which began the first of its three sessions on 4 February 1512. On an average over the years 1509 to 1515 Parliament met for one session each year.

The impression one gets of Henry VII's foreign policy is that, if possible, he would much rather have had no foreign policy at all; to him Britain was an island *off*, rather than *of* Europe, and if it was to become economically and politically stable it would have to remain so. Such a policy would have better served Henry VIII, but for him an active participation in the affairs of the continental powers and equal standing with the other members of the 'European Monarchs' Club' was the only way to greatness and preeminence. In 1511 he joined the Holy League of Pope Julius II, Ferdinand of Spain, the Emperor Maximilian and Venice with its aim of pushing French interests out of Italy, and agreed with Spain to make war on Louis XII before the end of April 1512.

Parliament was, therefore, summoned to find the money to enable the King to check 'the high and insatiable appetite' of the French King and 'the subtle, untrue, and crafty ymaginacion' of Henry's own brother-in-law, James IV of Scotland. Two more tenths and fifteenths were granted in this second Parliament's first session (4 February–30 March 1512) and one more in the second (4 November–20 December 1512), as well as a graduated tax on landed income, movables or wages.

Henry's victory at the Battle of the Spurs, and the defeat of James IV at Flodden Field in 1513, seemed, on the surface at least, some tangible return for the grants made to the King; but this was no more than a beginning and, having agreed with Ferdinand and Maximilian on a combined attack on France in 1514, Henry returned to the third session of this second Parliament (23 January–4 March 1514) wanting further supplies.

Of an elaborately graduated poll tax, calculated to bring in
£160,000, and of the taxes voted for his needs in 1514, no more
than a third had been collected by 5 February 1515, when Henry's
third Parliament assembled. War on the continent was out of
the question; Francis I, his predecessor's treaty with England
confirmed, and his agents stirring up trouble in Scotland to
keep England occupied, set off to pursue his ambitions in
Northern Italy.

There was the chance that Henry might stiffen resistance
to French aggrandizement by the distribution of subsidies, but
this would be an equally expensive alternative to direct military
action. A new general subsidy was proposed, and if that were
not enough a second subsidy should be levied, while any deficit
remaining was to be made up by the Speaker (Sir Thomas
Neville of Mereworth in Kent, a member of the King's Council,
who had been knighted by the King before the Lords and Commons when he had been officially presented), and other members
of the Commous meeting in council with the Chancellor, Treasurer
and the judges. A second subsidy was required and a tenth and
fifteenth.

It was not only financial troubles that concerned Parliament
at this time. In its first session it was greatly disturbed by the
Case of Richard Hunne, found hanged in the 'Lollards' Tower'
(the Bishop's prison at St Paul's) in 1514, and by the general
question of benefit of clergy, which was raised by this event.

Anticlericalism, an ally quickly enlisted by Henry in his attack
on Rome and the submission of the Church in England, was
already apparent in the House of Commons, and now the House
demanded the renewal of legislation, passed in 1512, which denied
benefit of clergy to clergy in minor orders. The Act was talked
out in the second session of Henry's third Parliament, nevertheless the Church had suffered a signal defeat, and Wolsey, who,
as a Cardinal, had assumed the headship of the English Church,
in this last session knelt in submission before an assembly of the
Council and both Houses of Parliament.

This episode is of great importance in our understanding of
Wolsey's attitude towards Parliament. If any reforms of the

Church were to be carried out, then he, and not a pack of meddling laymen in Parliament would see that they were. Clearly he held no brief for representative bodies like Parliament, for they were too critical of authority; and when he took over the Great Seal from Warham on 22 December 1515 – the day the King (at Wolsey's request) dissolved Parliament – it was clear that his predecessor's policy of regular consultation with Parliament would not be continued. During the time of Wolsey's power, from 1515 to 1529, Parliament met only once, in 1523, and the recesses before and after were the longest imposed on Parliament until the reign of Charles I and the so-called 'Eleven Years' Tyranny'.

Only sheer financial necessity compelled Wolsey to summon Parliament to meet at the Blackfriars on 15 April 1523. By that time his foreign policy, mistakenly designed to achieve international influence for England and international authority for himself, had fallen in shreds about his ears, so wildly was it out of keeping with England's real interests, so great a strain did it impose on the country's resources. The inept attempt to play off Francis I and the newly crowned Emperor Charles V against one another, the 'portentous deception' (Pollard) of the Field of Cloth of Gold, and the Anglo-Imperial alliance for the invasion of France deceived no one – least of all Francis and Charles – and the Emperor's former tutor, Adrian of Utrecht, beat Wolsey for the Papacy in 1522.

Forced loans, levied in the same year, could support no more than six months of war, even though they brought in some £350,000. With Charles V supreme in Italy and ready to launch his troops into Southern France, an English attack from the North might even be the means of restoring the Crown of France to Henry VIII. But such an impossibly archaic scheme needed money, which only Parliament could supply.

Wolsey anticipated no insuperable difficulties, nevertheless a sensible preliminary was to arrange for the Speaker of the Commons to be a man whom he trusted and could rely upon. Sir Thomas More, scholar, humanist, lawyer and Under-Treasurer of the Exchequer, seemed to be just that man. He was familiar with Wolsey's continental policy and, as a member of the Privy

Council since 1518, he had acted on affable terms as liaison between the Chancellor and the King. But Thomas More, unlike
Thomas Wolsey, was an honest man, and unlike Wolsey, he saw
clearly that the policy of war with France was a mistaken one; if
he could not approve of foreign conquest on moral grounds, as
Under-Treasurer he saw only too clearly the damaging effects
such a policy would have on the royal finances.

When the session opened Sir Thomas More as Speaker asked
that the members of the Commons be allowed to speak their
minds freely on all matters set before them – the first time the
Speaker had made such a request. 'Most gracious sovereign,' he
said,

considering that in your High Court of Parliament is nothing entreated
but matter of weight and importance concerning your realm and your
own royal estate, it could not fail to let and put to silence from the
giving of their advice and counsel many of your discreet Commons, to
the great hindrance of the common affairs, except that every of your
Commons were utterly discharged of all doubt and fear how anything
that it should happen them to speak should happen of your Highness
to be taken. ... It may therefore like your most abundant Grace,
our most benign and godly King, to give to all your Commons here
assembled your most gracious licence and pardon, freely, without
doubt of your dreadful displeasure, every man to discharge his conscience, and boldly, in everything incident among us, to declare his
advice; and whatsoever happen any man to say, that it may like your
noble Majesty, of your inestimable goodness, to take all in good part,
interpreting every man's words, how uncunningly so ever they be
couched, to proceed yet of good zeal towards the profit of your realm
and honour of your royal person, the prosperous estate and preservation whereof, most excellent sovereign, is the thing which we all, your
most humble loving subjects, according to the most bounden duty of
our natural allegiance, most highly desire and pray for.

His request was granted, and Wolsey can never have en-
visaged such a stormy passage as his financial demands received.
Perhaps it was More's presence that did the trick, a sign, as a
recent writer has rather oddly expressed it, 'that somewhere be-
neath that time-serving place-seeking jelly-like mass that the

Commons had become, a backbone was developing' (Philip Marsden, *The Officers of the Commons, 1363–1965*, Barrie & Rockcliff, 1966).

Wolsey paid two visits to the Commons in person on 29 and 30 April 1523 to make his demands. As war was now inevitable, a subsidy of £800,000 which represented four shillings in the pound of every man's lands or goods, was essential to pay for it. The Commons told him the demand was too heavy, so on his second visit Wolsey set out to bully the House into submission, claiming that the country could well afford to pay; to his intense anger and embarrassment the Commons, quite unmoved, retained 'a mervailous, obstinate silens'.

To have done otherwise, to have voiced their arguments then and there would have infringed their ancient liberty of debating only in private. The Speaker formally replied on the Commons' behalf, but here again he could make no proper answer as the form that that answer should take had not been arrived at by the Commons. Wolsey, therefore, retired discomfited, furious that More 'had not in this parliament in all things satisfied his desire'. The Commons were no less angry, criticizing particularly the King's policy of acquiring land in France, for Thérouanne, taken in 1513, had, they claimed, cost 'more than twenty such ungracious dogholes could be worth'.

On 13 May, after the matter had been 'debated and beaten xv or xvj dayes to gidder' the House agreed to vote supplies, but less than Wolsey had demanded. Wolsey was determined to have the full amount, and, having informed the Commons that the Lords had already agreed to it (in fact, they had not), the Court party within the Commons, led by Sir John Hussey, M.P. for Sleaford, set to work to secure the original grant. After agreement was reached on a proposal that landowners worth more than £50 a year should pay 1/- in the pound for a third year the House was prorogued on 21 May.

The debate continued in the second session, and was marked by a split between landowners and burgesses in the Commons over the proposal by the landowners that an extra grant of 1/- in the pound on goods should be paid in a fourth year. It was

More who brought the two sides together 'after long perswadying and privie laboryng of frendes', and agreement on the grant was reached. Continuing then with the discussion of 'common causes' the session ended on 13 August, by which time both the Speaker and the members themselves were tired out, the Parliament having continued for seventeen weeks.

Wolsey's subsequent actions illustrate his contempt for Parliament. So pressing were the demands for money made by the war with Scotland and the invasion of France that he completely overrode the Commons' stipulation that the grant they had agreed should be spread over a four-year period. In October 1523 Wolsey issued commissions to collect the grant all at once 'by anticipation'. It could not be done, however, and the Amicable Grant demanded of the laity and clergy in 1525 by prerogative alone was abandoned in the face of determined opposition from the country as a whole.

By November 1529, when Parliament next assembled for the first session of the long 'Reformation' Parliament, Wolsey was a doomed man, and the King's Matter, the so-called 'Divorce' Question, was running into such irritating opposition from the spiritual authorities that the King saw his best chance in a national combined attack upon the authority of Rome, which his former Chancellor had represented as papal legate, and which his own actions had done much to discredit, not least among those classes who sat as representatives of the counties and boroughs in the House of Commons.

The tone was set in the new Lord Chancellor's speech at the opening of Parliament, for the King, said Sir Thomas More,

considered how divers laws before this time were made now by long continuance and mutation of things very insufficient and unperfect, and also by the frail condition of man divers new enormities were sprung among the people, for the which no law was yet made to reform the same, which was the very cause why at that time the king had summoned this high court of parliament: and he resembled the king to a shepherd . . . for if the king be compared to his riches he is but a rich man, if a prince be compared to his honour, he is but an honourable man: but compare him to the multitude of his people and the number of his flock, then he is a ruler, a governor of might and puissance, so that his people maketh him a prince, as of the multitude of sheep cometh the name of a shepherd.

Straightway the Commons 'began to commune of their griefs wherewith the spirituality had before time grievously oppressed them'. Henry had grievances of his own against the spirituality, and in this community of interest, King and Commons, lay the strength of his position and the force of his policy. In fact, to carry out a policy at all Henry had to work with Parliament, and this he knew, for he was not just employing a complimentary turn of phrase in 1543 when he told the members 'We at no time stand so highly in our estate royal as in the time of Parliament, wherein we as head and you as members are conjoined and knit together into one body politic'.

The servants of the Tudor monarchy were drawn from the ranks of the vigorous middle class – in the towns the lawyers and merchants, the substantial yeomanry and prospering gentry in the counties, and in these 'new men' national loyalty and personal ambition combined so that their prosperity and that of the nation were bound up with the monarchy of Henry VIII.

Moreover, one salient characteristic of these men was their rugged anticlericalism. The restlessness of Richard Hunne and his friends was felt by others elsewhere than in London, east and south-east England especially, and it was fanned by the assorted writings of men like Simon Fish with his wild attack on the clergy in his *Supplication for Beggars*, and Christopher St German, a more constructive common lawyer, who passionately desired the abasement of all ecclesiastical jurisdiction, and firmly believed in the omnicompetence of the King-in-Parliament.

Papal interference in the country's affairs, the omnipresent financial demands of the Church, the coercive jurisidiction of the ecclesiastical courts, and the privileges and immunities of the clergy – all these aroused bad feeling and jealousy and offended a rapidly growing national selfconsciousness.

These sentiments (one might almost call them prejudices) were reflected and freely voiced in Parliament; that they could freely voice their opinions is shown by the fact that the clergy in 1515 had actually petitioned the King to ask if they could have the same freedom in Convocation as was enjoyed in Parliament, where, they claimed, members might attack the very laws of the country with impunity.

When the first session of the Reformation Parliament opened the Commons immediately appointed all the lawyers in the House 'to draw one bill of the probates of Testaments, another for Mortuaries, and the third for non-residence, pluralities, and taking of Farms by spiritual men', an attack on clerical privileges, which prompted John Fisher, the Bishop of Rochester, to remark 'in the parliament chamber these words: "my lords, you see daily what bills come here from the common house and all is to the destruction of the church; for God's sake see what a realm the kingdom of Bohemia was, and when the church went down, then fell the glory of the kingdom; now with the commons is nothing but down with the church, and all this, meseemeth, is for lack of faith only" '.

The Commons 'took the matter grievously' and sent a deputation of thirty members, led by their 'wise and discreet Speaker' Thomas Audley, to complain to the King that they 'which were elected for the wisest of all the shires, cities and boroughs within the realm of England, should be declared to lack faith, which was equivalent to say that they were as ill as Turks or Saracens'. When sent for Fisher explained to the King that he had meant that the Bohemians, not the Commons, lacked faith, but this 'blind excuse pleased the commons nothing at all'. Their attitude might be anti-clerical, but, they hastened to point out, it was certainly not heretical, although Kenneth Pickthorn has suggested that over and above this the significant reaction of the Commons on this occasion was against the implication inherent in Fisher's remarks that they had no competence to legislate in matters of faith and the Church.

The year 1529 is especially important in this story of the development of the Tudor Parliament, because it is a landmark in the story of the growing power of the House of Commons. 'The significant fact after all', wrote Conyers Read (in *The Tudors*, Oxford University Press, 1936) is that Henry should have turned to parliament. That in itself marks a definite break with Wolsey, indeed a definite break with the Tudor tradition up to that time. We have here the first expression of Henry VIII's definite acceptance of the principle of government by consent. It marks a turning point in English history, a turning point almost in the history of the western world, for had Wolsey's conception of government persisted England might have gone the way in which all the rest of Europe was to go, the way of absolute despotism. No matter if Henry packed his parliament or not, no matter if he completely dominated it. What mattered was that he made it an essential feature in his whole scheme of government. That was his great claim to distinction, perhaps his chief claim to be called great, and no preoccupation with his sex life and his multitudinous marriages ought to be allowed to obscure that fact. He was, as Professor Pollard has remarked, the greatest parliamentarian that ever sat on the English throne. That being so, it was well for the future of the world that he came just when he did, for at that precise moment the fate of popular government hung very precariously in the balance.

Further Reading

S. B. Chrimes, *Lancastrians, Yorkists and Henry VII.* Macmillan (London, 1964).

James Gairdner, *Henry VII.* Macmillan (London, 1889).

J. R. Lander, 'Edward IV: The Modern Legend: And a Revision', *History*, Vol. XLI, Nos. 141–3 (February–October 1956).

Kenneth Pickthorn, *Early Tudor Government: Henry VII.* Cambridge University Press (London, 1949).

A. L. Rowse, *Bosworth Field and the Wars of the Roses.* Macmillan (London, 1966).

B. P. Wolfe, *Yorkist and Early Tudor Government, 1461–1509.* Historical Association 'Aids for Teachers' Series, No. 12 (1966).

(See also pp. 129, 177–8.)

Principal Events, 1485—1529

1485. August. Death of Richard III at Market Bosworth
(Bosworth Field)
Accession of Henry Tudor, Earl of Richmond, as
Henry VII
November – March 1486: Henry's First Parliament

1486. January. Henry marries Elizabeth of York

1487. Lambert Simnel in Ireland claiming to be Edward, Earl of
Warwick
June. Battle of Stoke: Simnel, Lincoln and Lovell
defeated
November–December: Henry's Second Parliament

1488. English concern over French ambitions in Brittany

1489. *January–February 1490: Henry's Third Parliament*
February. Treaty of Redon with Anne of Brittany
March. Treaty of Medina del Campo with Spain

1490. Henry forms coalition against France

1491. *October–March 1492: Henry's Fourth Parliament*
Perkin Warbeck in Ireland claiming to be Richard, Duke of
York
December. Marriage of Anne of Brittany and Charles VIII
of France

1492. October. Henry invades France
November. Treaty of Étaples with France

1495. *October–December: Henry's Fifth Parliament*
November. Perkin Warbeck accepted as Duke of York by
James IV of Scotland

1496. *Magnus Intercursus* with the Netherlands

1497. *January–March: Henry's Sixth Parliament*
May. John Cabot sails from Bristol
Cornish Rising, provoked by taxation
June. Cornish Rising fails before London
July. Warbeck's cause abandoned by Scotland and Ireland
September. Warbeck lands in Cornwall, fails to take Exeter,
surrenders to Henry

1498. May. John Cabot's second voyage

1499. Erasmus first in England
      November. Execution of Warbeck and the Earl of Warwick
1501. November. Marriage of Henry's elder son, Arthur, and
      Catherine of Aragon
1502. April. Death of Prince Arthur
1503. June. Henry's second son, Henry, betrothed to Catherine
      August. Marriage of Henry's daughter, Margaret, to James
      IV of Scotland
1504. *January–April: Henry's Seventh Parliament*
1506. April. *Malus Intercursus* with the Netherlands
1507. Thomas Wolsey becomes a royal chaplain
1508. Sebastian Cabot sets sail
1509. April. Death of Henry VII
      Accession of Henry VIII at age 17
1510. *January–February: Henry's First Parliament*
1511. November. Henry joins Holy League of the Pope, Spain,
      Venice, England, against France
1512. *February–May 1514: Henry's Second Parliament*
1513. August. Henry invades France, expedition organized by
      Wolsey, Battle of the Spurs, Thérouanne and Tournai taken
      by Henry
1513. September. Defeat and death of James IV of Scotland at
      Flodden
1514. July. Wolsey becomes Archbishop of York
      August. Anglo-French Treaty, marriage of Henry's sister,
      Mary, and Louis XII
      December. Death of Richard Hunne in the 'Lollards' Tower'
1515. *February–December: Henry's Third Parliament*
      Pope Leo X makes Wolsey a cardinal
      December. Wolsey becomes Lord Chancellor on William
      Warham's resignation
1518. May. Wolsey created legate '*a latere*' ('from the Pope's side')
      October. Treaty of Universal Peace (the Pope, Emperor,
      France, Spain, England) directed against the Turk
1520. June. Field of Cloth of Gold
      Thomas Cromwell enters Wolsey's service
1521. Henry's *Assertio Septem Sacramentorum* ('A Defence of the

Seven Sacraments') against the views of Luther

October. Henry awarded the title *Fidei Defensor* ('Defender of the Faith') by Pope Leo X

Death of Leo X. Wolsey anxious to become Pope

1523. *April–August: Henry's Fourth Parliament*
Failure of Henry's second French campaign
September. Death of Pope Adrian VI. Wolsey again unsuccessful in his ambition to become Pope

1524. Henry concerned for the succession to the throne

1527. Beginning of the 'King's Great Matter'

1528. June. Pope Clement VII appoints Cardinals Campeggio and Wolsey to try the matter of the King's 'divorce'

1529. May. Cardinals' Court opens at Blackfriars

1529. July. Pope recalls King's case to Rome. Campeggio adjourns the Blackfriars Court
August. Thomas Cranmer suggests Henry appeal to the universities on the matter of the King's 'Divorce'
October. Wolsey indicted for praemunire. Resigns as Chancellor

1530. November. Wolsey arrested and ordered to London. Dies at Leicester

[8] FROM 1529 TO 1558

The Reformation Parliament

The Reformation Parliament was certainly not 'packed' and by
sixteenth century standards (though not by those of the nineteenth and twentieth centuries) it was roughly representative of
the nation. As in any other Tudor Parliament, the majority of
the members were either royal servants, or were linked in some
way with the Crown, or its ministers; but this does not mean
that it was a servile assembly.

This Parliament lasted for seven years, from 1529 to 1536, and
the total length of its seven sessions was almost eighteen months.
This means that it sat for longer than all the Parliaments of
Edward IV, or all those of Henry VII put together, and almost a
third longer than all the Parliaments held in the first twenty
years of Henry VIII's reign.

During its life it carried out 'a series of changes more pro-
found and widespread than any which had yet been accomplished
in the annals of English legislation'. The authority of Rome was
cast off, the Church was successfully nationalized under the
control of the Crown, the English Reformation was launched on
its unique course, and the principles which formed the basis of
the Elizabethan settlement of the Church were clearly set down.
Not that Henry VIII had for one moment intended that all this
should happen, because his real purpose in summoning this
Parliament was to bring the clergy to heel in case they should be
called upon to adjudicate in the matter of his 'divorce', and to
have at hand a means of blackmailing the Pope into issuing the
necessary dispensation, which would leave Henry free to marry
again and secure a legitimate succession.

In 1531 the clergy, under threat of praemunire, accepted
Henry as 'their singular protector, only and supreme lord, and
as far as the law of Christ allows also Supreme head'. Although
this added nothing to the King's authority it did serve to bring
the clergy firmly under his control; but Henry believed his title

to be *supremum caput in temporalibus*, therefore the spiritual supremacy of the Pope was not thereby denied and the break with Rome cannot, at this stage, have been in his mind. The continued intransigence of Rome, however, and the urgency of securing the succession forced him to sever the link that had been forged so many centuries before.

Nor did he envisage that his action would open the floodgates of Protestant thought, for he himself maintained throughout his reign an uncompromising orthodoxy. Cuthbert Tunstal, writing to the exiled Reginald Pole in 1536, made this quite clear:

You suppose that the King's grace . . . in taking upon him the title of Supreme Head . . . intendeth to separate his church of England from the unity of the whole body of Christendom . . . You do err too far. His full purpose and intent is to see the laws of Almighty God purely and sincerely kept and observed in his realm, and not to separate himself or his realm any wise from the unity of Christ's Catholic Church.

And the point was emphasized in the Act in Restraint of Appeals, the Act in Conditional Restraint of Annates, the Dispensations Act, and the *King's Book*. 'I am very sorry to know and hear', Henry himself complained towards the end of his reign, 'how irreverently that most precious jewel the word of God is disputed, rhymed, sung and jangled in every ale-house and tavern', and his last years were troubled by the attempts in the Act of Ten Articles of 1536, the new Heresy Act, and the Act of Six Articles three years later to hold back the torrent of Protestantism he had unwittingly released.

As for the royal supremacy, that was simply a restatement of what was the King's by the laws of God, and was, as Stephen Gardiner, Bishop of Winchester, wrote in his classic Tudor defence of the royal supremacy, *De vera obedientia*, '. . . no new thing. The Kings of Israel exercised it; so did the Roman emperors; so did the ancient Kings of England. To call the King Supreme Head in Earth of the Church of England is merely expressing an existing right in plain words.' Richard Sampson of Chichester's *Oratio*, published in 1533, and Richard Foxe's *De vera differentia* of 1534 echoed Gardiner's view.

Thomas Cromwell

If, in the first few years of the Reformation Parliament, Henry was uncertain as to how best to achieve his desires in the matters of his divorce and the succession, when Thomas Cromwell, 'the most devoted, laborious and efficient servant of the Crown in the long history of England', as Professor Dickens describes him, became a member of the King's Council, his policy was vigorously directed towards the destruction of papal jurisdiction and the complete withdrawal of England from obedience to Rome.

Thomas Cromwell had re-entered Parliament in 1529 (he had previously been a member of the 1523 Parliament) intent, as we have seen, on making a name for himself – 'he trusted shortly to be better regarded or [i.e. before] all was done'. As a member of Wolsey's household he had been in daily contact with ambitious, yet indolent clerics, and, as a self-made man, he resented their easy success, while as a shrewd man of business he was contemptuous of their wealth and inefficiency; and this coloured his attitude to the Church when he was a member of Parliament.

In the Commons he made a thorough study of its work and procedure, thus familiarizing himself with the great potential of this assembly as an instrument of national policy. By 1532 he was already attracting the attention of his contemporaries by his wide knowledge and remarkable industry, and was winning the confidence of the King by his preparation of the final draft of the Supplication against the Ordinaries and by his inclusion in the Act 'concerning the restraint of payment of annates' of a clause postponing its implementation until the King should decide.

Any assessment of Cromwell's contribution to the work of the Reformation Parliament and the accomplishment of what amounted to a revolution in Church and State must be based upon the researches of Dr Elton, although it must be noted that some of his arguments, notably his claim that 'Cromwell, not Henry, was really the government' (*The Tudor Revolution in Government*, Cambridge University Press, 1953), have been convincingly challenged by other scholars. (See R. B. Wernham's review of Dr Elton's book in the *English Historical Review* (January 1956), and 'A Revolution in Tudor History? Dr Elton's Interpretation of the Age' by Penry Williams in *Past and Present* (July 1963).)

Cromwell, says Dr Elton, introduced the King to the potentialities of statute in furthering the attack on Rome. In the first nine sessions of Parliament, spread over the first twenty-two years of Henry VIII's reign, 203 Acts were passed, 148 of them public; but in the eight years of Cromwell's ministry, from 1533 to his fall in 1540, in eight sessions of Parliament, 333 Acts were passed, of which 200 were of general importance and greatly influenced by Cromwell himself.

Comparison with the 45 years of Elizabeth's reign and 13 sessions of Parliament, in which only 79 more Public Acts were passed than in Cromwell's ministry is equally striking. Also, in sheer volume in the *Statutes of the Realm* Cromwell's statutes are impressive.

Statute, for Cromwell, was supreme, for it brought together, as Cromwell put it, 'Your Royal Majesty and your Lords Spiritual and Temporal, and Commons, representing the whole state of your realm in this your most High Court of Parliament', a most formidable combination as both clergy and Papacy were to find out to their cost.

Cromwell was not a Machiavellian; he was not aiming at a despotism, and the charge that he was is largely based on the personally hostile and prejudiced testimony of Reginald Pole. Like St German, whose writings may well have influenced him, Cromwell believed in the legislative supremacy of the King-in-Parliament. The 'divers good laws and statutes' passed between 1532 and 1534 enveloped the skeleton of royal supremacy like quick-drying cement – 'a technical triumph in the field of legislation'. 'In our long history', writes Professor Dickens,

no changes so momentous have ever been accomplished by statute within three years. Never before had a block of legislation so extensive and so closely coordinated passed through Parliament. Never had one step led so smoothly to another; never had lobbying been so effectively conducted; never had loopholes for opposition been closed with such remorseless efficiency. Once again the Crown was back under business management. After the gorgeous international advertising of Wolsey and the flounderings of lesser men [i.e. Norfolk and Gardiner], the ghosts of Empsom and Dudley were enjoying a belated laugh. The new managing director had severed all connection with the big continental combine: he had even presumed to make a subsidiary firm of *ecclesia anglicana*. This severance and this merger had their convenience; indeed, they defined most prophetically some of the main features of English life in the centuries to come.

Of the two Houses of Parliament the Lords were the easier to control. Thirteen sees became vacant between 1529 and 1536, and many abbeys fell vacant about 1533, so that Henry was able to put in his own nominees; when spiritual lords like Gardiner, who had favoured the 'divorce', realized in 1534 that far more was really intended, the lack of support from their peers demonstrated that their protests had come too late. Likewise the lay lords; for the career of Wolsey had alienated any sympathy they might have had for the Church and the clergy, and there was a sporting chance that they could play jackal to Henry's lion if the wealth of the Church was plundered.

The House of Commons had, as we have seen, a community of interest with the policy of the King and Cromwell, but not all the legislation of the Reformation Parliament was allowed through without opposition. The first draft of the Statute of Uses of 1532 ran into opposition when 'many froward and wilful persons, not regarding what might ensue would neither consent to the bill as the Lords had agreed and set their hands, nor yet agree to no reasonable qualification of the same'. Whereupon the King met a delegation from the Commons and himself assured them that' if you will not take some reasonable end now when it is offered, I will search out the extremity of the law and then will I not offer you so much again'.

The Act in Restraint of Appeals, though carefully tailored by Cromwell to call attention to definite abuses, met with considerable opposition, although Chapuys, the Imperial ambassador to England, maintained that this was only a mercenary reaction, prompted by the fear that such a step might cause other countries, out of respect for the Pope, to break off their trade with England.

Also the Treasons Act, introduced in the November–December session in 1534, which rendered any denial of the royal supremacy punishable by death, had its passage through the Commons disputed; 'there was never more sticking at the passage of any Act than at the passing of the same', wrote a contemporary; while the Act of Proclamations of 1539, by which the King and Council 'may set forthe at all tymes by auctoritie of this Acte his proclamacions' was resisted by both Houses.

There was, therefore, considerable point in attempting some management of the Commons by influencing elections to secure for the King what Cromwell in 1539 called a 'never more tractable Parliament'. Certainly from the time of Edward IV the Crown had cultivated a pro-Crown, pro-Government interest in the Commons, and in the 1523 Parliament opposition to a money grant was only overcome, after a great deal of argument, by the preponderance in the House of 'King's servants'.

In 1534 Cromwell was assessing the merits of various Members and thinking in terms of bye-elections, and in 1536 he went the whole hog (although the episode is an isolated one) in managing the Canterbury election. Two members had already been returned before the Sheriff, John Hobbys, was informed of the King's and Cromwell's preference for someone else. He begged to be excused and for the election to stand. In his reply Cromwell expressed unreasonable surprise that the Mayor, Sheriff and Commonalty of Canterbury had chosen

other at your own wills and minds contrary to the King's pleasure and commandment in that behalf . . . wherefore, in avoiding further displeasure that might thereby ensue, I require you on the King's behalf that notwithstanding the said election ye proceed to a new and elect those other, according to the tenor of the former letters to you directed for that purpose, without failing so to do as the King's trust and expectation is in you and as ye intend to avoid his Highness' displeasure at your peril.

Two days later the Mayor, Sheriff and Commonalty of Canterbury wrote that the King's wishes had been fulfilled 'freely with one voice and without any contradiction'.

Perhaps the extent to which Cromwell and the Crown influenced elections was exaggerated, both in the sixteenth century and since; but it is significant that the assembly of the Pilgrimage of Grace at Pontefract in 1536 included in its demands a 'Reformation for the election of knights of the shire and burgesses', and in protesting at royal nominations of burgesses claimed that 'The old custom was that none of the King's servants should be of the commons house; yet most of that house were the King's servants'.

The Pilgrimage was crushed, and other 'blatant electoral devices', as Sir John Neale calls them, were employed by Cromwell and other royal councillors in 1539. In March of that year Christopher More wrote to Cromwell:

My lord admiral has showed me that your pleasure is to have a friend of yours to be one of the burgesses of the Parliament for the borough of Gatton in the shire of Surrey, whereof Sir Roger Copley is owner; wherein your lordship shall have your pleasure . . . I had promised it unto a friend of mine, which, since I know your lordship's pleasure, at my desire is contented to leave it. So that now, if I might know the name of your lordship's friend, I shall send it to Mr Copley to the intent that he may cause the indentures to be made between the sheriff and him for the same.

For choosing a burgess for Farnham the Earl of Southampton 'picked out certain of the best of the country whose names be in the schedule herewith sent, to the intent ye [i.e. Cromwell] shall prick his head whom you would have chosen'.

Sir Edmund Knyvet left Cromwell an equally free choice in selecting knights of the shire for Norfolk, for at the time of election (1539) he declared he would not 'fail to be in readiness with such my tenants and friends as I can make there, to give my voice and consent with all my company unto any such as by your lordship shall be ensigned me; doubting no deal but that I . . . shall cry so loud on him that the voice of the other shall ill be heard'.

Should any bold or turbulent spirit find his way into the House of Commons – 'if any such there shall be, as I think there shall be few or none', Cromwell assured the King that he had 'appointed your Majesty's servant Mr Morison' to be a member, for 'no doubt he shall be ready to answer and take up such as would crake or face with literature of learning or by indirect ways'.

By sixteenth-century standards Cromwell was simply doing what was expected of a King's minister – the fact that he did it so much better than anyone else is what has drawn attention to it.

Cromwell was also keenly aware of the power of the press to support the King's policy, and during the course of his ministry he conducted a remarkable propaganda campaign – some 50 books, most of them published by the King's printer, or by printers under the influence of the Crown. These books, by Thomas Starkey, Richard Sampson, Edward Fox, Richard Morison and Richard Taverner, and other members of Cromwell's literary circus, were required to demonstrate that the royal supremacy was founded upon tradition and was justified in both ancient and medieval theory. The doctrines of Marsiglio of Padua, the medieval doctor and theologian, who had published his *Defensor Pacis* in 1324 in praise of the secular state and against the pretensions of the Church, were especially relevant; and in 1535, another of Cromwell's authors, William Marshall, published the first English translation of the *Defensor Pacis*, with notes which contained many references to the essential role of Parliament in the State.

Finally, the seven years' life of the Reformation Parliament had important social effects. Naturally enough, during so long a Parliament, its members got to know one another very well indeed, and family alliances, which otherwise would hardly have been formed, resulted, as we have seen, from the increased social intercourse among M.P.s. What is more important, perhaps, is that they got to know the ways of Parliament very well, too – its legislative procedure, and, above all, its absolute indispensability, for this Parliament had 'developed a sense of continuity and a claim in legislation and a voice in national policy' (Rowse) which its successors never forgot.

For the House of Lords, too, this was an important period in its development. Writs of summons were now being sent to all lay lords on the principle of their hereditary right rather than

simply by royal selection, and to all the professional councillors
and officials; but the Act of Precedence, passed in 1539 'for the
precedence of the lords in the parliament chamber', by enacting
that anyone holding the 'offices of Lord Chancellor, Lord Treasurer,
Lord President of the King's Council, Lord Privy Seal, or Chief
Secretary', if he is 'under the degree of a Baron of the Parliament
. . . can have no interest to give any assent or dissent in the said
House', ensured that the Lords became exclusively a body of
peers of the realm. Privy Councillors below baronial rank, mere
'assistants' after 1539, found their place now in the House of
Commons, while the law officers and judges, with the exception
of the Chancellor, who was sometimes created a peer, found their
place in the courts.

This placement of royal officials in the Lower House illustrates,
not only the growing importance of the Commons, but also the
continuing concern of the government to keep it firmly under its
control. Thus when Thomas Wriothesley and Ralph Sadler
were made principal secretaries early in April, 1540, they were
exempted from the terms of the Act of Precedence so that they
could sit in the Parliament that assembled on 12 April as members
of the Commons, on purpose to perform more useful service for
the King than was possible if they had sat in the House of Lords.

Six days later Thomas Cromwell was made Earl of Essex and
High Chamberlain of England; within a month he was lodged
in the Tower, his royal master now well able to manage without
him, throwing him to his enemies just as he had done Wolsey.
The charges made against him were so absurd that Cromwell's
enemies chose to proceed (as did Strafford's enemies in 1640) by
Act of Attainder, which precluded his making any defence.
Having received three readings in the Lords between 17 and 19
June, the Bill of Attainder was sent to the Commons; a revised
bill was sent back to the Lords (but not until 29 June), which
received the Lords' approval and the King's assent on the same
day.

'He suffered death', wrote Sir Edward Coke, 'by a law which
he himself had made', for he had drafted the Act of 1534 which
had increased the range of treason. He had exalted the power of

Parliament, and it was Parliament which had now interpreted the charges against him as constituting treason. Cromwell himself made no complaint. 'I am a subject', he said when the Bill of Attainder was passed, 'and born to obey laws, and, knowing that the trial of all laws only consisteth in honest and probable witness, and considering that the state of your whole realm had heard and received them, and that they have proceeded, as I am sure they have done, without malice, I submitted me to their sentence'.

Henry's last years, 1540–7

On 12 July 1540 Henry's distasteful Cromwell-inspired marriage to Anne of Cleves was annulled by Act of Parliament after it had been agreed 'in full Convocation' that they 'were no wise bound by the marriage solemnized between them', and the clergy's representatives had duly reported their findings to the Lords and Commons. Parliament then petitioned Henry 'for the good of his people' to marry again, but within two years, on the fourth day of the Parliament which met on 16 January 1542, a first reading was given to a bill attainting Henry's latest wife, Catherine Howard, of treason. Henry suggested that Catherine should go down to Parliament and defend herself in person, but she declined the offer; agreed by the Lords, on 8 February the bill was passed to the Commons and dealt with so promptly that on 11 February the Chancellor produced this bill, together with a statute covering proceedings against 'traitors' who, like Lady Rochfort, had lost their reason.

Lest a public ceremony should renew the King's quite hypothetical grief the request of a committee of both Houses that Henry should give his royal assent by letters patent, which were 'of as good strength and force as though the King's person had been there personally present and had assented openly', was, in fact, granted. Then the Commons joined with the Lords, so that 'in the presence of each house and of the whole council of parliament, the said statutes might receive the force and authority of law; which was done'. This marked the beginning of the practice whereby the royal assent was given to Acts of Parliament by a commission acting on the Crown's behalf.

After Cromwell's death, reverting to an almost Wolseyesque foreign policy of continental involvement, Henry's financial demands of Parliament were regular and large; matters were made worse by the deepening economic instability of his later years, a situation which the sale of the land acquired by the dissolution of the religious houses between 1536 and 1540 could not resolve.

The argument and uncertainty over religion was a further cause of uneasiness to both the King and his people. The break with Rome had unintentionally, but inevitably, encouraged the freer expression of those reforming tendencies in matters of doctrine, which Henry himself was prepared to accept only up to a point; for, in spite of the Bible in English and the English services, Henry remained, in doctrine, Catholic to the last, and the Six Articles were the clear manifestation of this determination to apply (albeit too late) some effective brake to the Reforming movement.

For national unity could not be achieved if there was unrestrained religious disunity. At the end of the parliamentary session in 1545 it was this situation, mirrored in Parliament, which moved Henry to address the Lords and Commons in person, in place of the Lord Chancellor, who was 'not able so to open and set forth my mind and meaning, and the secrets of my heart, in so plain and ample manner, as I myself am and can do'. He acknowledged the love and harmony that so far had existed between himself and his Parliament, but it could not continue unless both Houses made up their minds 'to amend one thing, which surely is amiss and far out of order ... Which is, that Charity and Concord is not amongst you, but Discord and Dissension beareth rule in every place.' The clergy preached against one another, the laity spoke out in criticism of them all, and 'that most precious jewel, the Word of God, is disputed, rhymed, sung and jangled in every Ale-house and Tavern'.

'Therefore,' he concluded, '. . . be in charity one with another like brother and brother; love, dread, and serve God; to which I, as your Supreme Head and Sovereign Lord, exhort and require you; and then I doubt not but that love and league, that I spake of in the beginning, shall never be dissolved or broke betwixt us.'

In spite of this appeal Henry knew well that religious dissension could not be allayed by a simple appeal; but the bond with Parliament remained. He had, in fact, succeeded 'in creating in the English mind an attitude of loyalty to his dynasty strong enough to carry through all the distractions of Edward's and Mary's reigns and to find its supreme expression in the universal devotion to his second daughter, Elizabeth' (Conyers Read, in *The Tudors*, Oxford University Press, 1936).

Henry VIII's last Parliament was ended on 31 January 1547 with the announcement of his death three days earlier.

Edward VI, 1547-53

Henry's will had made no provision for a Protector, although his son, Edward, was only nine years old when he became King in 1547; but the late King's executors, who now constituted themselves as the Privy Council, elected one of their number, the Earl of Hertford, Edward's uncle, Protector of the Realm and governor of the King's person. He was Protestant and Protestants dominated the Council. For two years and nine months Hertford, or the Duke of Somerset as he became in 1547, ruled England in Edward's name, pursuing a policy of moderation and 'too much gentleness'.

By the Treasons Act of 1547 the treason and heresy laws of Henry VIII were repealed, along with the Act of Six Articles, all restrictions on reading and expounding the Scriptures – in fact 'all the Acts of Parliament and Estatutes touching, mentioning, or in any wise concerning religion or opinions'. Protestant exiles returned, along with foreign reformers like Martin Bucer, John A'Lasco and Peter Martyr, all eager to forward the Reformation for, although Somerset was not prepared to order change, yet he was quite ready to authorize it.

Within a liberal system of government he followed a religious policy of toleration and compromise. The First Prayer Book of 1549, agreed to by Crown, Council and Parliament, is the product of this attitude, just as the Second Prayer Book of 1552 is a product of the latter part of the reign from 1549 when, having brought about Somerset's overthrow, the Earl of Warwick (he became Duke of Northumberland in 1551) replaced liberalism by severity and forced on the country more religious changes in three years than it had experienced in the twenty years since Wolsey's downfall.

Parliament, which was frequently called, offered little in the way of opposition, but as the gentry who controlled the Council were also the dominant force in Parliament, and as the Council prepared the bulk of the legislation, this is hardly surprising; in fact, in February 1553, a month before Parliament met, a small Committee of the Council – a sort of inner Council – was named 'to consyder what lawes shalbe established in this Parliament'.

Opposition came in economic matters where the private and class interests of members baulked legislation; as was the case in 1547, when three bills dealing with enclosure were introduced by John Hales of Coventry, a minor government official and champion in Parliament of the Commonweal, or Commonwealth party, were rejected, and their cause countered by the enactment of the savage Act of 1547, which demanded that vagabonds be branded 'in the breast' and reduced to slavery.

Very little attempt was made by Somerset to influence parliamentary elections. Before his first Parliament, which met on 4 November 1547, letters were sent by the Privy Council to the Lord Warden of the Cinque Ports and the Sheriff of Kent to attempt to secure the election of a Privy Councillor and prospective Speaker, Sir John Baker; but they aroused local resistance and so were almost apologetically followed up by letters to assure the Sherriff that 'they meant not nor mean to deprive the shire by any their commandment of their liberty of election whom they should think meet . . . nevertheless if they would in satisfaction of their Lordships' request grant their voices to Mr Baker they would take it thankfully' – Mr Baker, however, sat in that Parliament for Huntingdon, and not Kent.

By contrast, Northumberland had no such scruples, nor such finesse, and his interference was blatant. In 1551 the Lord Chancellor was directed to enquire how many members had died since the last session, 24 November 1549 to 1 February 1550, 'to the intent that grave and wise men might be elected to supply their places, for the avoiding of the disorder that hath been noted in sundry young men and other of small judgement', and in bye-elections in 1552 at Reading and in Surrey and Hertfordshire the Council asked for the election of its own nominees.

Whatever the outcome this Council interference did not lead to a subservient assembly, for in the next session beginning 23 January 1552 the Commons passed a Treasons Bill ensuring that no one else would be put to death by the same procedure as that employed against Somerset; declined to proceed with a bill for Bishop Tunstall's attainder on a charge of treason, and rejected, or refused to consider a dozen bills, which Edward VI had drafted himself.

A more determined effort was made with elections for the second Parliament of the reign, which assembled in March 1553. All sheriffs were instructed to ensure that in electing representatives 'there be good regard had that the choice be made of men of gravity and knowledge in their own countries and towns', and 'that where our Privy Council, or any of them within their jurisdictions in our behalf shall recommend men of learning and wisdom, in such case their directions be regarded and followed, as tending to the same which we desire – that is, to have this assembly to be one of the most chiefest men in our realm for advice and good counsel'.

As a result, some fifteen or sixteen seats, perhaps, were filled as the Council wished, and the creation, or restoration of 22 boroughs (several of them insignificant Cornish ones) returning 44 members, was, in theory at least, a step in the same direction. But this Parliament was no more amenable, and the members returned for the half dozen Cornish boroughs were certainly not the 'yes men' Northumberland must have hoped they would be.

Without doubt Northumberland's government had alienated the conservative and more politically conscious members of Parliament, so that he could either get no money at all from Parliament, as in 1552, or just a little, and that very begrudgingly, as in 1553; and his pseudo-Protestant zeal aroused the mistrust of the zealous Protestants who were his best supporters. It was hardly likely that Northumberland's brazen plan to usurp the succession would find parliamentary approval, so after the brief session of 1553 Parliament was dissolved.

Mary, 1553–8

Mary came to the throne on a wave of popular emotion and loyal support, just as the Catholic James II was to do some 130 years later, and this carried over into the first Parliament of her reign, which sat from October to December 1553.

Parliament had assisted Henry VIII in carrying out a revolution; therefore, only by Parliament could that revolution be undone, as Mary now intended it should be. The ecclesiastical legislation of Edward VI's reign was repealed, and in doctrine and worship the clock was turned back to 1547, and the first stage of Mary's counter-Reformation was complete. Both Parliament and the Council, however, made it quite clear that they would not tolerate the restoration of ecclesiastical property, in which after all they held a vested interest; nor did they want the Queen to drop the title, or exercise of the royal supremacy over the Church.

Her second Parliament, from April to May 1554, restated their position; bills against heresy were defeated, and the clergy's petition for a restoration of ecclesiastical jurisdiction was also unsuccessful. Clearly the emotional Tudor spell was already rubbing off; the country was divided in faith, the hated Spanish alliance had aroused parliamentary opposition and precipitated Wyatt's Rebellion, while the Queen for 'the restitution of God's honour and glory' required that her country should be reconciled with Rome, which would mean a further step back in time to 1529, if not 1509.

Understandably, therefore, the writs for the election of a third Parliament in 1554 were accompanied by a letter from the Queen to all sheriffs, requiring that they should admonish the constituencies to choose representatives who should be 'of their inhabitants, as the laws require, and of the wise, grave and Catholic sort; such as indeed mean the true honour of God, with the prosperity of the Commonwealth'. This would appear to be a sign that the country gentry, who were increasingly entering Parliament as borough members, were proving to be something of a handful as far as government was concerned.

Nevertheless, when Parliament met in November it conceded more than its predecessors had done; by the second Act of Repeal the clock was turned back to 1529; the Act of Absolution from the Sin of Schism was given parliamentary authority. But Parliament would not budge on the matter of the restoration of ecclesiastical property, and of the monasteries dissolved by Henry VIII only Westminster, Sion, Smithfield and Greenwich were recalled to life, and that by the Queen's own return of secularized property. The heresy laws of Richard II, Henry IV and Henry V were restored, and Mary, exasperated by the (to her) inexplicable contumacy of so many of her subjects, clerical and lay, began to purge their heresy in the fires at Smithfield; Parliament regretted its action.

'None but Catholics and none who are suspect' the sheriffs were instructed to return to the autumn Parliament of 1555, but it was no good; Mary's policy, like Northumberland's before her, had stirred up opposition both in Parliament and outside, and this fourth Parliament, with 'many violent opposition members', proved the most obstreperous of all.

Only one subsidy would the Commons vote, instead of the subsidy and two-fifteenths actually asked for, and the government's desire to restore the payment of first-fruits and tenths to Rome was emphatically refused. 'After great disputes and contention . . . from daybreak, when they met, until 3 p.m.', while the door of the Commons' Chamber was locked from the outside 'no one being allowed egress either to eat or for any other purpose', the Commons gave a third reading to a bill, which freed the clergy from liability to pay first-fruits, but authorized the payment of tenths to the Papal Legate instead of the Crown; it further provided that, while the Queen could surrender her own revenue from these sources if she so wished, lay impropriators could pay if their consciences pricked them.

Having been locked in their own chamber the Commons were roused to show their defiance of the government by proceeding to lock themselves in while they rejected a bill against political and religious refugees overseas. The Queen's government retaliated by imprisoning in the Tower Sir Anthony Kingston, the man who had actually locked the Chamber door, together with the Sergeant-at-Arms, who had given him the key, and thus demonstrated a fine disregard for the privileges of the Commons' House.

When the Queen tried to secure to the Crown the right to enforce the attendance of members of the Commons (the Crown had actually started proceedings in the Queen's Bench against 33 members who had withdrawn from the 1554 Parliament 'when they saw the majority was inclined to sacrifice everything to the Ministry'), and to insist that boroughs should return townsmen as M.P.s instead of the obviously cantankerous country gentlemen, the Commons replied in kind by tacking to this bill a place bill of their own, which would have excluded all Crown servants from House of Commons membership. The bill was thrown out, of course, but the episode illustrates the total breakdown of the mutual understanding between Crown and Parliament, which had been achieved by Henry VIII, and which was to be rediscovered by Elizabeth.

Mary's last years were, for her, saddened by her husband's callous desertion, her failure to bear the longed-for child, and her complete inability to realize that her lineage, not her faith, had been the reason for her early popularity. For England these years brought anger and frustration as English interests took second place to those of Spain, as Calais was lost, as more simple, but sincere, Protestants were consigned to the flames.

Sir David Lindsay Keir (in *The Constitutional History of Modern Britain, 1485–1937*, Black, 1947) has suggested that as a result of Mary's failures, an anti-Roman and anti-clerical lead from a new sovereign would be immediately popular, and that the spirit of the people in 1558 was very like that in 1529. 'As in 1529', he writes, 'Parliament would concentrate and express it. Translated into action, it would move more swiftly and radically than in 1529, since the path of ecclesiastical revolution was now a familiar one, and the goal could easily be defined by reference to points attained in the past. All that was needed was a government prepared, as in 1529, to make a reversal of policy.'

Further Reading

J. J. BAGLEY, *Henry VIII*. Batsford (London, 1962).

BARRETT L. BEER, 'The Rise of John Dudley, Duke of Northumberland', *History Today*, Vol. XV, No. 4 (April 1965).

S. T. BINDOFF, 'A Kingdom at Stake, 1553', *History Today*, Vol. III, No. 9 (September 1953).

JOHN BOWLE, *Henry VIII*. Allen & Unwin (London, 1964).

HESTER W. CHAPMAN, *The Last Tudor King*. Jonathan Cape (London, 1958).

A. G. DICKENS, *Thomas Cromwell and the English Reformation*. English Universities Press, 'Teach Yourself History' Series (London, 1959).

G. R. ELTON, *Henry VIII*. Historical Association Pamphlet, General Series, No. 51 (1962).

G. R. ELTON, 'King or Minister?: The Man Behind the Henrician Reformation', *History*, Vol. XXXIX, No. 137 (October 1954).

G. R. ELTON, 'Thomas Cromwell', *History Today*, Vol. VI, No. 8 (August 1956).

G. R. ELTON, 'The Political Creed of Thomas Cromwell', *Transactions of the Royal Historical Society*, 5th Series, Vol. 6 (1956).

JOEL HURSTFIELD, 'Was there a Tudor Despotism after all?', *Transactions of the Royal Historical Society*, 5th Series, Vol. 17 (1967).

ERNESTO LANDI (trans. Maurice Cranston), 'The Political Philosophy of Macchiavelli', *History Today*, Vol. XIV, No. 8 (August 1964).

KENNETH PICKTHORN, *Early Tudor Government: Henry VIII*. Cambridge University Press (London, 1934).

H. F. M. PRESCOTT, *Mary Tudor*. Eyre & Spottiswoode, 2nd ed. (London, 1952).

A. L. Rowse, 'Eminent Henrician: Thomas Wriothesley, First Earl of Southampton', Part I *History Today*, Vol. XV, No. 6 (June 1965). Part II *History Today*, Vol. XV, No. 7 (July 1965).

H. R. Trevor-Roper, 'England's Moderniser: Thomas Cromwell', in *Historical Essays*. Macmillan (London, 1957).

R. B. Wernham, G. R. Elton's *Tudor Revolution in Government* (review). *English Historical Review* (January 1956).

(See also pp. 177–8.)

Principal Events, 1529—58

1529. *November–April 1536: Henry's Fifth Parliament (The 'Reformation' Parliament)*
Parliamentary attack on abuses in the Church – non-residence, plurality, sanctuary, probate, mortuaries

1530. November. Death of Wolsey
December. Clergy accused en bloc of breach of praemunire for accepting Wolsey as legate

1531. January. Henry forbidden to remarry by Pope Clement VII
February. Convocation of Canterbury buys its pardon
Convocation of York buys its pardon
Beggars' Act
Thomas Cromwell becomes Privy Councillor

1532. March. Commons' Supplication against the Ordinaries – an attack on clerical jurisdiction
May. The Submission of the Clergy. Sir Thomas More resigns as Lord Chancellor
August. Death of William Warham, Archbishop of Canterbury
Act in Conditional Restraint of Annates

1533. January. Henry marries Anne Boleyn. Sir Thomas Audley becomes Lord Chancellor
March. Thomas Cranmer consecrated Archbishop of Canterbury
Act in Restraint of Appeals
May. Cranmer pronounces Henry's marriage to Anne to be valid
June. Anne Boleyn crowned Queen
September. Henry excommunicated by the Pope. Princess Elizabeth born

1534. Act for the Submission of the Clergy
Act in Absolute Restraint of Annates
Dispensations Act
First Succession Act, confirming Henry's marriage to Anne and settling succession on her issue
March. The Pope decides in Catherine's favour

November. Oath of Succession sanctioned in Second Act of
Succession
Act of Supremacy
Act Annexing First-fruits and Tenths to the Crown
Treasons Act

1535. January. Cromwell appointed Vicar-General. Enquiry into
values of beneficiaries begins
June. Execution of Bishop Fisher of Rochester
July. Execution of Sir Thomas More. General Visitation
of the Monasteries begins
September. The *Valor Ecclesiasticus*

1536. January. Death of Catherine of Aragon
March. Act for the Dissolution of the Lesser Monasteries
May. Execution of Anne Boleyn. Cranmer declares her
marriage to Henry invalid. Henry marries Jane Seymour
June–July: Henry's Sixth Parliament
July. The Ten Articles
August. Cromwell issues the Injunctions
October. The Pilgrimage of Grace

1537. January. The Council of the North established
September. The 'Bishops' Book'
October. The birth of Prince Edward. Death of Jane Seymour
November. Proclamation banishing Anabaptists

1538. Destruction of images and the shrine of Thomas Becket

1539. Introduction of 'Matthew's Bible' (the 'Great Bible')
April–July 1540: Henry's Seventh Parliament
Act for the Dissolution of the Greater Monasteries
Act of Six Articles
October. Marriage treaty with Cleves

1540. January. Henry marries Anne of Cleves
March. The last abbey – Waltham Abbey – surrenders
to King
June. Cromwell arrested
July. Henry's marriage annulled by Convocation and
Parliament. Cromwell executed
August. Henry marries Catherine Howard

1542. *January–March 1544: Henry's Eighth Parliament*
February. Catherine Howard executed on charge of treason

November. Scots defeated at Solway Moss
December. Birth and accession of Mary, Queen of Scots

1543. May. The 'King's Book' published
July. Henry marries Catherine Parr

1544. War with France

1545. June. The English Litany
November–January 1547: Henry's Ninth Parliament

1546. June. Peace of Camp with France.

1547. January. Death of Henry VIII. Accession of Edward VI
Edward Seymour, Earl of Hertford, made Protector and
Duke of Somerset
September. Somerset defeats Scots at Pinkie
November–April 1552: Edward's First Parliament
Act for the Dissolution of the Chantries

1548. June. Proclamation against Enclosures

1549. First Act of Uniformity. First Book of Common Prayer
June. Rising in West Country against the Prayer Book
July. Kett's Rebellion
October. Somerset deposed. Replaced by John Dudley,
Earl of Warwick

1551. July. Treaty of Angers with France. Edward betrothed to
Elizabeth of France
October. Warwick becomes Duke of Northumberland

1552. January. Somerset executed
Second Act of Uniformity. Second Book of Common prayer

1553. *March: Edward's Second Parliament*
June. The 42 Articles. The King's 'Devise'. Lady Jane Grey
named next in succession
July. Death of Edward VI. Lady Jane Grey proclaimed
Queen. Northumberland's support disappears
August. Mary enters London
October. Mary pledged to Philip of Spain
October–December: Mary's First Parliament
First Statute of Repeal

1554. January. Sir Thomas Wyatt's Rebellion
February. Execution of Lady Jane Grey
April–May: Mary's Second Parliament
July. Marriage of Mary and Phillip

November–January 1555: Mary's Third Parliament
November. Cardinal Pole returns to England. England
reconciled to Rome
Act reviving the Heresy Laws
Second Statute of Repeal
1555. February. Burning of Protestants begins
October. Burning of Ridley and Latimer
October–December: Mary's Fourth Parliament
1556. March. Burning of Cranmer
1557. June. England involved by Philip in war with France
1558. January. Loss of Calais
January–November: Mary's Fifth Parliament
November. Death of Mary and Cardinal Pole

The Queen

In the afternoon of 30 November 1601, 'about three of the clock, some seven score of the House met at the great chamber before the Council Chamber in Whitehall. At length the Queen came into the Council Chamber, where, sitting under the cloth of state at the upper end, the Speaker with all the company came in, and after three low reverences made [he delivered his speech] . . . And after three low reverences made, he with the rest kneeled down, and her Majesty began thus to answer herself, viz

Mr Speaker, you give me thanks, but I doubt me I have more cause to thank you all than you me; and I charge you to thank them of the House of Commons from me, for had I not received a knowledge from you, I might have fallen into the lap of an error only for lack of true information. Since I was Queen yet did I never put my pen to any grant but that upon pretext and semblance made unto me that it was both good and beneficial to the subjects in general, though a private profit to some of my ancient servants who had deserved well. But the contrary being found by experience, I am exceeding beholden to such subjects as would move the same at first. And I am not so simple to suppose but that there be some of the Lower House whom these grievances never touched; and for them I think they speak out of zeal to their countries, and not out of spleen or malevolent affection as being parties grieved; and I take it exceeding grateful from them, because it gives us to know that no respects or interests had moved them other than the minds they bear to suffer no diminution of our honour and our subjects' love unto us. The zeal of which affection tending to ease my people and knit their hearts unto me, I embrace with a princely care; for above all earthly treasure I esteem my people's love, more than which I desire not to merit. . . . I have ever used to set the last judgment day before mine eyes, and so to rule as I shall be judged to answer before a Higher Judge. To whose judgment seat I do appeal, that never thought was cherished in my heart that tended not to my people's good . . . And although you have had and may have many princes more mighty and wise sitting in this seat, yet you never had or shall have any that will be more careful and loving. . . .

And so I commit you all to your best fortunes and further counsels. And I pray you, Mr Controller, Mr Secretary, and you of my Council, that before these gentlemen depart into their countries you bring them all to kiss my hand.

This extract from Elizabeth's 'Golden Speech', delivered in the last session of her last Parliament, contains the key to an understanding of her whole reign, for here was personal monarchy – not despotism – with much, if not everything, depending upon the personality of the monarch, the head of both Church and State.

Elizabeth, 'the choicest artist in Kingcraft that ever handled the sceptre in this northern climate', personified England in a quite remarkable and special way, for 'she was of God specially sent and ordained', and in the eyes of her people 'our God in earth'. Although her course was often erratic 'she brought England through a very perilous passage into smooth waters' (Conyers Read); on her life depended both the unity and the safety of England, its only real safeguard against the wiles of Mary, Queen of Scots, against Spain and the massing forces of the Counter Reformation, and it was from this that stemmed the mighty confidence and conceit, which characterized her reign.

The fact that her subjects worshipped her this side of idolatry also runs as a theme through her relationship with Parliament; for the Puritans, the growing force in the House of Commons, they in particular conceived a sincerely romantic attachment to the Queen. 'It makes my heart leap for joy to think we have such a jewel', declared one Puritan member, 'it makes all my joints to tremble for fear when I consider the loss of such a jewel'; and Job Throckmorton, a fiery Puritan newcomer to Parliament in 1586, who may indeed have been 'Martin Marprelate', earnestly wished that 'If it so pleased God the last day of Elizabeth's life might be the last day of this earth'.

This cult of Elizabeth contained a great deal that was artificial, yet it was essentially sincere, and the view recently expressed that Elizabeth 'was served up so much [flattery] by her "faithful Commons" that even she was frequently disgusted with them. Small wonder that she treated them invariably like

idiot children – they almost begged for contempt' (Philip Marsden, *The Officers of the Commons, 1363–1965* Barrie & Rockcliff
1966), is hopelessly wide of the mark. Underlying the repeated
collisions that occurred through divergence of temperament and
policy between Elizabeth and her Parliaments was 'a strange,
fundamental harmony' (J. E. Neale, in *Elizabeth and Her Parliaments, 1584–1601*, Cape, 1957), although this did place the
Commons in a continual dilemma, well illustrated by the com-
ment of a diarist when members were confronted with a pro-
hibitory message from the Queen: 'Either they must offend their
gracious Sovereign, towards whom . . . they dared not so much as
to lift one evil thought or imagination; or else to suffer the
liberties of their House to be infringed'. This, together with the
great ability, and, above all, the quite remarkable personality
of the Queen, ensures a royal success that, for the same reasons,
was altogether denied to James I.

The Church Settlement

On 12 February 1559 Sir Anthony Cooke, sometime tutor to
Edward VI and but lately returned from exile in Strasbourg,
informed Peter Martyr that 'We are busy in Parliament about
expelling the tyranny of the pope and restoring the royal authority'; the result of this activity was the Elizabethan Church
Settlement, a settlement not so conservative as Elizabeth had
wished, but as comprehensive as it was possible in the circumstances to make it.

To achieve this the Queen had made, as Sir Nicholas Throckmorton advised, 'a discreet beginning', preferring a gentle
moderation to the frenzies of some of the wilder spirits inside and
outside Parliament; for, as Armagil Waad wrote in *The distresses
of the Commonwealth, with the means to remedy them,* 'Glasses
with small necks, if you pour into them any liquor suddenly or
violently, will not be so filled. . . . Howbeit, if you instil water
into them by a little and little they are soon replenished.'

Elizabeth's original intention was that an interim settlement
should be arranged, which would do no violence to the Catholic

faith and would secure the support of some of the bishops, while moderate reformers would be selected to fill the vacant sees. A new Oath of Supremacy would indicate the out-and-out Papists, and then a Convocation, made up of Catholic and Protestant moderates could produce a Prayer Book, which would embody the comprehensive aims of the Queen and bring an early religious peace; Convocation, not Parliament, was to be the instrument of the settlement.

Elizabeth's hopes, however, were dashed by the opposition of the Marian Catholics and, above all, by the determined opposition in the House of Commons under the leadership of men like Sir Anthony Cooke and Sir Francis Knollys, who had the influential support of reforming divines like John Jewel, Edmund Grindal, Richard Cox, John Aylmer, Richard Sampson and John Scory. What the Commons wanted was a re-establishment of 'the religion used in King Edward's last year', and when the conclusion of the Peace of Câteau-Cambrésis with France removed the government's need for caution the interim plan collapsed; the government gave way to demands for an immediate Act of Uniformity and abandoned the hope that the Prayer Book of 1549 might be restored.

The Westminster Disputation was permitted during the Easter recess of Elizabeth's first Parliament, which met on 25 January 1559, but this was not the Convocation, which, after debate, should have decided the issue. When Parliament reassembled the Acts of Supremacy and Uniformity reviving the Edwardian Settlement were passed, and it was the second, not the first of Edward's Prayer Books, which was prescribed, although only after a few significant alterations had been made at the Queen's insistence.

But if the Church Settlement was satisfactory, or, at least acceptable, to the broad middle band of moderate opinion, there were on the left and the right dissident extremists – Puritans and Catholics, whose views, in fact, could never have been reconciled. The Catholics, although the object of exaggerated and quite irrational mistrust, constituted no real danger, either to the Church Settlement (in spite of the Jesuits and the Seminarists), or to the State (in spite of the Bull of Excommunication and the Spanish threat, which dissolved in 1588); on the other hand, the Puritans of the lunatic fringe were a danger, both to the Settlement, whose whole character they were determined to change, and to the State, whose essential unity they threatened to destroy. Moreover, Puritan influence in the House of Commons was strong and actively vociferous, especially when the fear of Roman machinations made Protestant patriotism and anti-Catholic feeling run high; such times occurred between the arrival of Mary, Queen of Scots, in the North of England in 1568, and the Papal Bull excommunicating Elizabeth and releasing her Catholic subjects from allegiance in 1570; in 1580, when the Jesuits reinforced the Seminarist Movement in England; in 1584, when Protestant Europe was inflamed (and terrified) by the murder of William the Silent, and whenever the zeal of Walsingham revealed the details of another Catholic plot against the life of the Queen.

Elizabeth, however, was a *politique* and hated religious enthusiasm, and consistently defended her Church Settlement against determined Puritan inroads. In the parliamentary sessions in the spring of 1571 and the summer of 1572 she was forced to prevent the Commons passing religious legislation that would have radically altered the Settlement of 1559.

William Strickland, M.P. for Scarborough, undoubtedly the spokesman for a group of determined Puritans in the House, and author of a proposal to reform the Prayer Book, was briefly suspended in 1571 'for exhibiting a bill into the House against the prerogative of the Queen'. In the next session she suppressed a debate on measures which might well have restricted the application of the Act of Uniformity to those 'who shall use any manner of superstitious or papistical service', yet would have left Puritan ministers free to change at will the form of worship this Act had prescribed. Her action was decisive: the offending bills were impounded and the Speaker warned the Commons that 'her Highness' pleasure is that from henceforth no bills concerning religion shall be preferred or received into this House, unless the same should be first considered and liked by the clergy'.

In the parliamentary session of 16 January to 18 March 1581 Puritan sympathy among the gentry and their growing opposition to the bishops was once more demonstrated when articles for the 'reformation of Discipline in the Church' were delivered to the Queen. Having handed them over to Archbishop Sandys of York for his consideration, Elizabeth made sure that they were not returned to the M.P.s who had presented them, assuring Sandys that 'her Highness was sufficient of herself to deal with the clergy in matters ecclesiastical; and that the Parliament House should not meddle therein'.

By 1587, however, the Puritan cause was on the wane, and their preparations for the Parliament which met on 29 October 1586 indicate a mood of desperation. Doubtless their relentless agitation had lost them some support, as had their stricter 'classis' discipline; but they had also alienated the parliamentary Erastians, who, though they had cashed in on Puritan discontent to extend their own control in ecclesiastical affairs, saw nothing attractive in the substitution of a rigid Calvinistic system for the rule of bishops; as well as the supporters of the royal supremacy, who, being devoted to the principle of obedience to constituted authority in both Church and State, were alarmed by the extreme violence of Puritan claims. Archbishop Whitgift expressed their feelings perfectly when he said: 'Wherein differ these men, in this case, from the Papists? The Pope denieth the supremacy of princes: so do, in effect, these.'

When Anthony Cope, the zealous Puritan who sat for Banbury introduced 'a Bill and a Book' in February 1587, providing for the abolition of episcopacy, the introduction of Presbyterian discipline and the Genevan Service Book, the Commons responded coolly; the bill was not, in fact, read, and the Speaker reminded the House that 'her Majesty before this time had commanded the House not to meddle with this matter'.

Elizabeth had not forgotten; the 'Bill and a Book' was confiscated and Cope and his supporters lodged in the Tower. Elizabeth had defeated the last serious Puritan political campaign; Parliament became less unruly and the tension between Queen and Parliament eased at the end of the reign, thus averting the clash that would inevitably have occurred had there been a Puritan victory.

Freedom of speech

'The discussions in the English Parliament', wrote Henry VIII to the Pope, 'are free and unrestricted; the Crown has no power to limit their debates or to control the votes of the members. They determine everything for themselves, as the interests of the commonwealth require.' Theory and practice on this score, however, did not make for a happy marriage, and Elizabeth, like her Tudor predecessors (Henry VIII included), certainly regarded the Commons' privilege of free speech as having quite definite limitations.

At the opening of every parliamentary session she granted the Speaker's customary demand 'that the assembly of the Lower House may have frank and free liberties to speak their minds without any controlment, blame, grudge, menaces or displeasure, according to the old ancient order', yet she forbade the House of Commons to discuss matters within the royal prerogative, 'matters of state', like the succession, foreign policy, and, as we have seen, 'causes ecclesiastical', but allowed them to discuss 'other matters concerning the commonwealth' – trade and enclosures.

In general these restrictions on the House of Commons were accepted by the gentry who dominated Parliament, as devotion to the Queen meant the assurance of property; nevertheless, with men like the staunch Puritan Peter Wentworth, who took his brother Paul's place in Parliament in 1571, devotion to the Queen, great though it was, came second to their love of liberty, and freedom of speech was an essential ingredient of that liberty.

In Elizabeth's reign we see the inexorable progression from the demand for freedom of speech to the right actually to initiate policy, which in the early seventeenth century so exacerbated relations between Crown and Parliament that it turned them into a conflict. When, in the debate on the Queen's marriage and succession in 1566 the House was told to proceed no further 'in their suit, but to satisfy themselves with her Highness's promise of marriage', Paul Wentworth, 'Wentworth the Wrangler', 'moved whether the Queen's commandment was not against the liberties'; whereupon the Queen, through the Speaker, again commanded that 'there should not be further talk of that matter', Clearly Elizabeth was greatly angered by the growing influence within the Commons of the 'broachers and workers', a small number of 'unbridled persons whose mouth was never snaffled by the rider'.

The Commons, however, construed her commands as implying not only a lack of duty on their part, but also that they deserved 'to be deprived' of 'an ancient laudable custom, always from the beginning necessarily annexed to our assembly, and by your Majesty always confirmed: that is, a leeful sufferance and dutiful liberty to treat and devise of matters honourable for your Majesty and profitable for your realm'. Indeed, they assured her, such a 'yoke of commandment' was 'unnecessary, unaccustomed' and 'undeserved'.

Reluctantly realizing that Parliament was, in fact, a necessary evil, the Queen, in a display of tact and skilful playing upon the vanity of the Commons, withdrew her commands and remitted a third of the subsidy she so badly needed; but when the House attempted to use (as they had done in 1563) the preamble to a subsidy bill as a vehicle of propaganda by including her promises to marry and determine the succession, Elizabeth disciplined them severely, and, on 2 January 1567, dissolved Parliament, certain that no future general election could produce a more intolerable assembly; for, observed D'Ewes, 'Mr Paul Wentworth and others used so great liberty of speech as (I conceive) was never used in any Parliament or session of Parliament before or since'.

The 'liberty of the House', however, continued as the rallying cry for the members of the Commons. It aroused the demand that William Strickland, who had been suspended from Parliament by the Privy Council for introducing into the Parliament of 1571 a bill 'for reformation of the Book of Common Prayer', should be heard at the bar of the House. Sir Francis Knollys,

Treasurer of the Household, denied that Strickland had been 'stayed for any word or speech by him in that place offered, but for the exhibiting of a bill into the House against the prerogative of the Queen, which was not to be tolerated'.

The Puritan lawyer, Christopher Yelverton, a fellow-member with 'Strickland the Slinger' of the 'choir' of active, noisy members in the second session of the 1566 Parliament, and so described in a lampoon of that time, regarded this as a perilous precedent, which, under a less gracious prince, 'might be construed as of duty and enforced even on this ground of the present permission. He further said, that all matters not treason, or too much to the derogation of the imperial Crown, were tolerable there, where all things came to be considered of, and where there was such fulness of power as even the right of the Crown was to be determined ... He shewed it was fit for princes to have their prerogatives; but yet the same to be straitened within reasonable limits. The Prince, he shewed, could not of herself make laws; neither might she by the same reason break laws'. The next day Strickland resumed his place in the Commons.

With Peter Wentworth 'liberty of free speech' was also a recurrent, because dominating, theme. 'Amongst other', he told the Speaker at the opening of the second session of the 1572 Parliament on 8 February 1576, 'two things do great hurt in this place. ... The one is a rumour which runneth about the House, and this it is, "Take heed what you do; the Queen's Majesty liketh not such a matter; whosoever preferreth it, she will be offended with him": or the contrary, "Her Majesty liketh of such a matter; whosoever speaketh against it, she will be much offended with him". The other: sometimes a message is brought into the House, either of commanding or inhibiting, very injurious to the freedom of speech and consultation. I would to God, Mr Speaker, that these two were buried in hell, I mean rumours and messages, for wicked undoubtedly they are; the reason is, the devil was the first author of them, from whom proceedeth nothing but wickedness. ... It is a dangerous thing in a prince unkindly to abuse his or her nobility and people. ... And how could any prince more unkindly intreat, abuse, oppose herself against her nobility and people than her Majesty did the last Parliament? . . . And will not this her Majesty's handling, think you, Mr Speaker, make cold dealing in any of her Majesty's subjects towards her again? I fear it will. . . . And I beseech . . . God to endue her Majesty with his wisdom, whereby she may discern faithful advice from traitorous, sugared speeches.' Wentworth, however, did not have the full support of the House, and it was on its orders that he was put into the Sergeant's ward and was sent to the Tower 'for the extenuating of his fault' by a committee specially set up by the Commons.

As far as the government, and indeed many of the M.P.s were concerned, the great problem was where to draw the line between freedom of speech and the abuse of that freedom. Sir William Mildmay, Chancellor of the Exchequer and Privy Councillor, put this concern into words on 12 March 1576, the day Wentworth was released and made his submission on his knees to the House; what he said had a specific relevance:

True it is [he said] that nothing can be well concluded in a council where there is not allowed, in debating of causes brought in, deliberation, liberty, and freedom of speech; otherwise, if in consultation men be either interrupted or terrified, so as they cannot nor dare not speak their opinions freely, like as that council cannot but be reputed for a servile council, even so all the proceedings therein shall be rather to satisfy the wills of a few, than to determine that which shall be just and reasonable. But herein we may not forget to put a difference between liberty of speech and licentious speech; for by the one men deliver their opinions freely, and with this caution, that all be spoken, pertinently, modestly, reverently and discreetly; the other contrariwise, uttereth all impertinently, rashly, arrogantly and irreverently, without respect of person, time or place: and though freedom of speech hath always been used in this great council of parliament, and is a thing most necessary to be preserved amongst us; yet the same was never nor ought to be extended so far, as though a man in this House may speak what and of whom he list. The contrary whereof, both in our own days and in the days of our predecessors, by the punishment of such inconsiderate and disorderly speakers, hath appeared.

But Wentworth was a Puritan, his house at Lillingstone Lovell in Buckinghamshire, according to his bishop, a centre for

Puritan worship for the whole neighbourhood, and his championship of free speech in Parliament was designed to help the Puritan cause; if complete freedom of speech were won in the House of Commons then no longer would the Queen be able to resist the attacks of the Puritans upon the Church as established in 1559.

Elizabeth, however, kept the upper hand. When she stopped the attempt in the Commons to reform the Church on Presbyterian lines in the Parliament of 1586–7, Wentworth, claiming she had again infringed the rights of the House, drew up a series of questions, the answers to which he intended should be regarded as definite rulings of the House. The questions were never, in fact, put, and for taking part in 'conferences in matters of religion', which, being held outside Parliament, were not protected by privilege, Wentworth and four others – Sir Anthony Cope, Edward Lewkenor, Ranulf Hurleston and Robert Bainbridge – no doubt at the instigation of the Queen, were sent to the Tower.

In 1594, when Wentworth was again in the Tower for preparing a campaign to attack the Queen in Parliament if she failed to declare the name of the heir to the throne, he wrote an answer to Father Robert Persons's *Conference about the Next Succession to the Crown of England*, criticizing the Jesuit for over-exalting Parliament; but the questions Wentworth had framed in 1587 did just that, and so are important as demonstrating the radical view of the supremacy of Parliament.

These were some of these questions:

Whether this Council be not a place for any Member ... freely ... by bill or speech, to utter any of the griefs of this commonwealth, whatsoever, touching the service of God, the safety of the prince, and this noble realm? ... Whether there be any council which can make, add to or diminish from the laws of the realm, but only this council of parliament? ... Whether the Speaker or any other may interrupt any member of this council in his speech? Whether the Speaker may rise when he will, any matter being propounded, without consent of the House, or not? ... Whether the Speaker may overrule the House? ... Whether it be not ... against the law that the Prince or Privy Council should send for any Member ... and check, blame, or punish

them for any speech used in this place, except it be for traitorous words?
... Whether it be not against the ... liberties of this House to receive
messages either of commanding or prohibiting? ... Whether the
Prince and State can ... be maintained without this Council of
Parliament, not altering the government of the State?

Yet in spite of Wentworth and the minority of members who
actually supported him, the final judgment on what, for all
practical purposes, constituted freedom of speech was that of the
Queen, and this view she clearly expressed in the Lord Keeper's
reply to the Speaker's petition for privileges in 1593, and this she
maintained against all opposition throughout her reign:

Mr Speaker, if any shall deliver to you any bill that passeth the reach
of a subject's brain to mention, that same you receive but not with
purpose to shew it where it best becometh you. Next, if any speech
undecent or matter unfit for that place be used, remember them of
this lesson. Your petitions ... must be ruled, and that her Majesty
granteth you liberal but not licentious speech, liberty therefore but
with due limitation. For even as there can be no good consultation
where all freedom of advice is barred, so will there be no good conclusion where every man may speak what he listeth ... It shall be
meet therefore that each man of you contain his speech within the
bounds of loyalty and good discretion, being assured that as the contrary is punishable in all men, so most of all in them that take upon
them to be counsellors and procurators of the commonwealth. For
liberty of speech her Majesty commandeth me to tell you that to say
yea or no to bills, God forbid that any man should be restrained
or afraid to answer according to his best liking, with some short
declaration of his reason therein, and therein to have a free voice,
which is the very true liberty of the House; not, as some suppose, to
speak there of all causes as him listeth, and to frame a form of
religion or a state of government as to their idle brains shall seem
meetest.

Freedom from arrest

The claim by both Houses to freedom from arrest in civil actions
– the claim did not include treason, felony, or breach of the peace
– was a most ancient one. With the lay and spiritual peers the

immunity was 'for ever sacred and inviolable', but with the Commons it only applied during the time that the House was actually sitting and for 'a reasonable time' before and after the assembly of Parliament. In Martin's Case in 1587 the Commons preferred to hedge on the question of what constituted 'a reasonable time'; it meant 'a convenient time', they said, and Martin's arrest twenty days before the beginning of Parliament was considered within that period, although they took no proceedings against the man who had arrested him as he could hardly be expected to know, if the Commons did not, that twenty days 'would be taken for reasonable time'.

Henry VIII had vigorously supported this privilege for the Commons in 1543 over the case of George Ferrers, who was imprisoned as surety for a debt during a parliamentary session. The case is important because Ferrers was released by the Commons on their own authority, and the officials who opposed his release were punished for contempt.

By the end of the century the right of the House to take independent action to enforce this privilege was accepted when, in Fitzherbert's Case in 1593, the Sergeant-at-Arms brought Fitzherbert from prison to the bar of the House. In 1576 the Sergeant-at-Arms had also acted at the Commons' direction in the case of Edward Smalley, a servant of Arthur Hall, M.P. for Grantham, because the privilege of members was deemed to extend to their servants as well.

The cases of James Digges and Robert Finnies in 1584, and of William Hogan in 1601 illustrate the same claim made by the House of Lords, whose agent on such occasions was the Gentleman Usher of the Black Rod.

Declining years after 1585

The reign of Elizabeth falls naturally into two parts. Up to c. 1585 she succeeded in preserving peace and confidently built up the support of the majority of her people. At home she counter-balanced the adventurous spirit of Leicester and the conservatism of Burghley; abroad she took no risks, apart from a

never-repeated invasion of France in 1562. Both at home and
abroad she employed delay as the main instrument of her policy,
believing that time alone could heal the old divisions and would
solve those vexing problems of her marriage, the succession, and
her attitude towards Spain, as indeed it did.

Although in frequent conflict with her Parliaments on matters
of policy, she was concerned to maintain good relations with her
subjects by ensuring that they understood and approved of her
actions. This she did through varied means of propaganda – her
own speeches, or those of royal officials at the opening or proroguing of Parliament; public hearings of the Court of Star
Chamber and the ecclesiastical courts; the Paul's Cross Sermon
and sermons on special occasions; prayers in churches, proclamations and declarations explaining and justifying her actions,
and which were prepared for both home and overseas consump-
tion; and by frequent progresses, which brought her into inti-
mate contact with her people.

But, above all, her success throughout was a triumph of tran-
scendant personality, uniting her people in the cult of the Virgin
Queen, on whom the security of the realm and the confusion of
the alien forces of the Counter Reformation depended.

After 1585, however, the situation had changed. Reluctant
involvement in war with Spain required parliamentary aid in
taxation, and the Parliaments of 1585, 1587, 1589, 1593, 1597 and
1601 were all asked for subsidies; the money was readily granted,
but the very fact that the Crown stood in need of extraordinary
grants made it especially vulnerable to any claim by Parliament
that it should know how the money was spent and should even
take a hand in the spending of it.

In 1601

The crown was deep in debt: Elizabeth owed the Corporation [of
London] £80,000, and had failed to pay the interest charges on the
last loan, and a further £120,000 was outstanding on privy seal loans.
Crown lands were being sold on an unprecedented scale and the
proceeds were being used, not to repay these debts, but to keep the
crown's head above the continuously high level of expenditure. Moreover, the queen was old, there were doubts about the succession, and

there was never any guarantee that her successor would honour her debts. These factors combined to produce a situation in which Elizabeth's credit reached its nadir. (R. B. Outhwaite, *Studies in Elizabethan Government Finance*, 1964).

There were other troubles in the 1590s besides financial difficulties: plague; bad harvests, caused by the exceptionally wet summers in 1594–7, and subsequent famine – 'One year', said a contemporary preacher, 'there hath been hunger, the second there was dearth, and the third there was a great cleanness of teeth'; prices continued to soar; there was social discontent and political discord as Essex's bold bid for personal power at the expense of the Crown ruined the equilibrium of the patronage system.

Recalcitrant M.P.s like Wentworth, Strickland, Norton, Saville, Hoby, Dalton, and Morice might be interviewed by the Queen and censured or imprisoned; the Queen by tactfully gentle answers might well turn away the Commons' wrath – 'the grace of pronunciation and of her apt and refined words, so learnedly composed', wrote one who was present at her 'Golden Speech' in 1601, 'did ravish the sense of the hearers with such admiration, as every new sentence made me half forget the precedents' – but the effect was only temporary.

The influence of the Privy Councillors continued to dominate Parliament for the whole of Elizabeth's reign. They made the first two speeches and the last in any discussion; they indicated the Queen's wishes, the attitude of the Lords; there were Privy Councillors on every Committee, and 'all the Privy Council of the House' served on important ones, which was really only reasonable when one remembers that they had a great advantage over M.P.s in matters of government in that they had the information to assess the national situation, where the ordinary member was familiar only with his local scene. This is not to belittle the value of experience in local government; indeed, it meant that the country gentry knew what legislation was needed to improve it – stopping up loopholes, perhaps, or strengthening the hands of the Justices of the Peace – and gave them an interest in the work of the several departments of national government, while their Puritanism and their desire to promote it made them tenacious adversaries.

In the last years of the reign the Privy Councillors found the Commons heavy going; measures they had introduced were delayed, or rejected, and Elizabeth in 1593 expressed dismay 'that such irreverence was observed towards the Privy Councillors, who were not to be accounted as common knights and burgesses of the House'. This was but a beginning; according to an anonymous observer, writing in the reign of Charles I, the real parliamentary counter-attack was made after 1601 when 'the Puritans began to spit out their venom against the Councillors'.

Sir John Neale concludes that the main achievement of the Elizabethan House of Commons was to increase the rate at which they were moving towards 'the winning of the initiative', by the better organization of their procedures in the House, and by developing 'the art of opposition, which might be considered the outstanding contribution of the Elizabethan period to parliamentary history'. One may also add that this period also saw the emergence of a diverse group of persuasive speakers, committed 'Parliament men': lawyers for the most part, men like Peter and Paul Wentworth, Arthur Hall, Thomas Norton, William Fleetwood, Thomas Digges, Sir Walter Raleigh, Robert Cecil and Francis Bacon, skilful in debate, men of wit and gifted oratory.

In spite of the fervour of the monopolies agitation in Elizabeth's last Parliament of 27 October to 19 December 1601, her last years were marked by an easing of the tension between the Crown and Parliament. The old glamour and glory still remained, if somewhat tarnished; but it was no longer valid, and many matters needed to be taken in hand – and Elizabeth realized this; but out of respect for the Queen, who had, indeed, when all is done, 'reigned with their loves', the Commons were prepared to withhold their aspirations to supremacy in Parliament and in the realm, but only until such time (and this they made clear in their Apology of 1604) as they should meet her successor.

Further Reading

B. W. BECKINGSALE, *Queen Elizabeth*. Batsford (London, 1963).

J. B. BLACK, *The Age of Elizabeth*. Oxford University Press, 'Oxford History of England', 2nd ed. (London, 1959).

JOEL HURSTFIELD, *The Elizabethan Nation*. B.B.C. Publications (London, 1964).

JOEL HURSTFIELD, *Elizabeth I and the Unity of England*. English Universities Press, 'Teach Yourself History' Series (London, 1960).

JOEL HURSTFIELD, 'England in the Year of Shakespeare's Birth, 1564', *History Today*, Vol. XIV, No. 2 (February 1964).

JOEL HURSTFIELD, 'Burghley: Minister to Elizabeth I', *History Today*, Vol. VI, No. 12 (December 1956).

JOEL HURSTFIELD, 'Robert Cecil, Earl of Salisbury', *History Today*, Vol. VII, No. 5 (May 1957).

GLADYS JENKINS, 'Ways and Means in Elizabethan Propaganda', *History*, Vol. XXVI, No. 102 (September 1941).

W. T. MACCAFFREY, 'Elizabethan Politics: The First Decade, 1558–1568', *Past and Present*, No. 24 (April 1963).

J. E. NEALE, 'The Elizabethan Age', in *Essays in Elizabethan History*. Jonathan Cape (London, 1958).

J. E. NEALE, *Queen Elizabeth*. Jonathan Cape (London, 1934).

J. E. NEALE, 'The Accession of Queen Elizabeth I', *History Today*, Vol. III, No. 5 (May 1953).

J. E. NEALE, *Elizabeth I and her Parliaments, 1559–1581*. Jonathan Cape (London, 1953).

J. E. NEALE, *Elizabeth I and her Parliaments, 1584–1601*. Jonathan Cape (London, 1957).

J. E. NEALE, 'The Via Media in Politics', in *Essays in Elizabethan History*. Jonathan Cape (London, 1958).

H. GARETH OWEN, 'Paul's Cross: The Broadcasting House of Elizabethan London', *History Today*, Vol. XI, No. 12 (December 1961).

A. L. ROWSE, *The England of Elizabeth: The Structure of Society*. Macmillan (London, 1950).

A. L. ROWSE, 'The Coronation of Queen Elizabeth I', *History Today*, Vol. III, No. 5 (May 1953).

A. L. ROWSE, 'Queen Elizabeth and the Historians', *History Today*, Vol. III, No. 9 (September 1953).

CHARLES WILLIAMS, *Queen Elizabeth*. Duckworth, 'Great Lives' Series (London, 1936).
PENRY WILLIAMS, 'The Fall of Essex', *History Today*, Vol. VII, No. 11 (November 1957). (See also pp. 177–8.)

Principal Events, 1558—1603

1558. November. Accession of Elizabeth I
William Cecil appointed Principal Secretary of State
1559. January, Coronation of Elizabeth
January–May: Elizabeth's First Parliament
March. Conference of Westminster
Act of Supremacy
Act of Uniformity
Recognition of the Queen's Title
First Act of Treason
December. Matthew Parker installed as Archbishop of
Canterbury
1560. July. Treaty of Edinburgh with France
1561. August. Mary, Queen of Scots, returned to Scotland
1562. September. Secret Treaty of Richmond signed with the
Huguenots. English troops occupy Le Havre
October. Elizabeth seriously ill with small-pox
John Hawkins enters African slave trade
1563. *January–January 1567: Elizabeth's Second Parliament*
Act for the Assurance of the Queen's Power
Act for the Relief of the Poor
Statute of Artificers
July. English withdrawal from Le Havre
1564. April. Treaty of Troyes with France
1565. July. Mary, Queen of Scots, marries Lord Darnley,
great-grandson of Henry VII
1566. March. Murder of Rizzio by Darnley and Scottish lords
June. Birth of James – son of Mary, Queen of Scots and
Darnley
Parker's *Book of Advertisements*
1567. February. Darnley murdered
May. Mary marries James Hepburn, Earl of Bothwell
June. Mary and Bothwell defeated by the Lords of the
Council at Carberry Hill. Mary captured, Bothwell escapes
to Denmark. Mary forced to abdicate in favour of her infant
son, James

1568. Mary escapes from Loch Leven Castle; is defeated at
Langside
Mary takes refuge in England
Mary transferred from Bolton to Tutbury, Staffordshire
William Allen opens seminary at Douai

1569. November. The Northern Rebellion

1570. February. Elizabeth excommunicated by Bull of Pius V,
Regnans in Excelsis

1571. February. Proposal for Elizabeth's marriage to Duke of
Anjou
March. Ridolfi's plot
William Cecil becomes Lord Burghley
April–May: Elizabeth's Third Parliament
Second Treasons Act
Act against the bringing in of Papal Bulls
Thirty-Nine Articles sanctioned by Parliament
(Subscription Act)
Puritan Cartwright's 'Admonition to Parliament'

1572. *May–April 1583: Elizabeth's Fourth Parliament*
Cartwright's 'Second Admonition'
Burghley appointed Lord Treasurer
July. Execution of Duke of Norfolk
August. The Massacre of St Bartholomew
Poor Relief Act

1573. May. Capture of Edinburgh Castle by English troops

1574. First seminary priests from Douai land in England

1575. May. Death of Archbishop Parker
Edmund Grindal tanslated from York to Canterbury

1577. Queen suspends Grindal from office for refusing to suppress
'Prophesyings'

1580. First Jesuit priests – Edmund Campion and Robert
Persons – land in England
September. Francis Drake returns from circumnavigation of
the globe (set out 1577)

1581. Campion caught and executed
Act against Reconciliation to Rome

1583. July. Death of Archbishop Grindal; succeeded at Canterbury
by John Whitgift
Throckmorton's Plot

1584. January. Spanish Ambassador, Mendoza, ordered home
July. Murder of William of Orange
The 'Bond of Association' formed
November–September 1585: Elizabeth's Fifth Parliament
1585. January. Parry's Plot
Act for the Surety of the Queen's Person
Act against Jesuits and Seminary Priests
December. Mary, Queen of Scots taken from Tutbury to
Chartley Manor. Earl of Leicester's expedition to the
Netherlands
1586. July. Treaty of Berwick between England and Scotland
August. Babington's Plot. Mary, Queen of Scots implicated
October. Mary removed to Fotheringay to face trial
October–March 1587: Elizabeth's Sixth Parliament
1587. February. Execution of Mary, Queen of Scots at Fotheringay
April. Drake raids Cadiz
Martin Marprelate Tracts against the Bishops
First establishment of Virginia by Sir Walter Raleigh
1588. July. The Spanish Armada in the English Channel.
Decisive battle off Gravelines
1589. *February–March Elizabeth's Seventh Parliament*
1593. *February–April: Elizabeth's Eighth Parliament*
Act against Popish Recusants
Great Subsidy Debate in Parliament
1596. June. Successful attack on Cadiz led by the Earl of Essex
October. Second Spanish Armada dispersed off Cape Finisterre
1597. October. Third Spanish Armada dispersed off Blavet
October–February 1598: Elizabeth's Ninth Parliament
1598. Act for Relief of the Poor
Act for Punishment of Rogues and Vagabonds (Beggars Act)
Act for erecting of hospitals and workhouses
August. Death of Lord Burghley
1599. January. Essex appointed Lord Lieutenant in Ireland
September. Essex returns to London
December. Foundation of the East India Company
1601. February. Rebellion and execution of the Earl of Essex
October–December: Elizabeth's Tenth Parliament
Debate on Monopolies
Act for the Relief of the Poor
1603. March. Death of Elizabeth I

[10] CROWN AND PARLIAMENT, 1603–29

The Scottish Solomon

At about three o'clock on the morning of 24 March 1603 Queen Elizabeth 'departed this life, mildly like a lamb, easily like a ripe apple from the tree', and the succession passed to her cousin, James VI of Scotland. Elizabeth had reigned for too long; the Tudor system, although it survived for another forty years, in the last decade of her reign was showing unmistakable signs of collapse, and this 'marking-time' period, when no remedies were being supplied for existing grievances, was bound to make things even more difficult for her successor. And James VI of Scotland, James I of England, was not at all the man for the occasion.

Not all of his difficulties were of his own making. He was a foreigner, with no experience or understanding of the English system of government and the English governing classes, the ruler of a country, which, to Englishmen at least, was quite barbaric; and he was a man. The chivalry, which had undoubtedly softened the demands and tempered the moods of the House of Commons in Elizabeth's declining years, now ceased, and James was seen, just as he was, with none of the aura of majesty and mystery, which had transformed Elizabeth into 'Gloriana'. Nor was the contrast offered by James a pleasing one to eyes that were essentially, and naturally, critical; for though his personal appearance and disgusting habits were, to say the least, unprepossessing, he was by upbringing and background quite unsuited for the tricky balancing act he ought really to have performed.

He had been King of Scotland since 1567 – for as long as he could remember – and by 1603, in his thirty-seventh year, his own ideas of kingship had been fully formed, and were, at his age, unlikely ever to be changed, or with such as James, ever even modified. He had spent his childhood under the domination of a triumphant Kirk, and his Presbyterian tutors, Peter Young and George Buchanan, had drummed into him the doctrine that

kings existed by the will and for the good of the people; the
people were the authors of kings, they must, therefore, be also
authors of the law, which it was the king's duty to preserve,
administer and obey. By his coronation oath the King agreed a
solemn contract with his people to fulfil his duties to them faithfully, and if he did not do this then he became a tyrant, and as
such could be brought to task by his subjects, who could impose
a punishment of deposition, or even death.

As so often happens in such circumstances James's own views
on the subject of the role and authority of the monarch developed
on lines very different from those prescribed by his Kirkomaniac
tutors. Although there are frequent references in his writings
and speeches to fundamental law and the advisability of governing according to law, for him constitutional kingship had no
appeal whatsoever; far more congenial were the absolutist ideas
of the French political philosopher, Jean Bodin, then current at
the Court of the French King Henry III, which James had
readily imbibed from Esmé Stuart, Seigneur d'Aubigny, who had
arrived in Scotland in 1579, and had gained complete ascendancy
over the young King's mind.

It was, therefore, to counter the political doctrine inherent in
Scottish Calvinism that James formulated his own claims of
sovereignty: for the Divine Right of the Kirk he substituted the
Divine Right of Kings; to the popular sovereignty and right of
resistance propounded by Buchanan, Melville and Knox, he
preferred monarchical sovereignty and the duty of passive resistance; where the Kirk claimed omnipotence, James claimed to
be, in the words of the English Act of Supremacy of 1559,
'supreme in all things or causes as well spiritual as temporal'.

A King, James believed, is God's representative on earth, and
for all his actions his responsibility is to God alone. His power
came into being before there were any forms of government or
law, so it was from him that all institutions, all laws are derived.
As the author of all law he is bound to be above all law, and as
for Parliament, 'which is nothing else but the head court of the
King and his vassals', its part in legislation is entirely subordinate; for, although the King can legislate without Parliament,

'yet it lies in the power of no parliament to make any kind of law or statute without his sceptre be to it, for giving it the force of a law'. Thus the King is 'overlord of the whole land ... master over every person that inhabiteth the same, having power over the life and death of every one of them'.

These sweeping claims James made in his *True Law of Free Monarchies*, written for the benefit of the heir to the Scottish throne, and published anonymously in 1598, and no change in situations or conditions during his reign in England caused him to moderate his views in any way. 'The State of monarchy', he told Parliament in 1609, 'is the supremest thing on earth: for kings are not only God's lieutenants upon earth, and sit upon God's throne, but even by God himself they are called Gods'; and in 1616, in a speech in Star Chamber, he declared: 'It is atheism and blasphemy to dispute what God can do ... so it is presumption and high contempt in a subject to dispute what a king can do, or say that a king cannot do this or that; but rest in that which is the king's revealed will in his law.'

This stubborn inflexibility was one of the chief causes of the constitutional struggle that was to defeat James and destroy his son. Another was his Scottish experience. James's record as King of Scotland was an impressive and successful one; for he humbled his 'over-mighty subjects', resisted the claims of the Kirk, and established a strong centralized monarchy – just as the Tudors had done in England. Unfortunately, he believed that this experience would guarantee his success in England, and he entered his new kingdom, therefore, positively overflowing with paternal wisdom and benevolence and notions of government, which, by now in the English context, were hopelessly out of date and unrealistic, and certain to arouse hostility; in particular from two great English institutions – Parliament and the Common Law, both formidable opponents, because, as he and Charles I were to find out for themselves, they were invincible.

If James lacked Tudor tact and understanding, he also lacked their uncanny skill in choosing the right men for their service. James 'could criticize a theory but he could not judge a man' (W. S. Holdsworth, *History of English Law*, Methuen, 1938);

he could not tell a wise man from a fool, nor a rogue from an honest man. Not that there was any lack of brilliant men around him – Francis Bacon, the intellectual turned politician, Lionel Cranfield, and, carried forward, as it were from Elizabeth's reign, Robert Cecil – but they never enjoyed the full confidence of the Crown, James preferring to be manipulated by the Spanish ambassador, Gondomar, and those sleazy adventurers and political nincompoops Robert Carr, Earl of Somerset, and George Villiers, Duke of Buckingham; where the Tudors had governed by patronage James ruled by favouritism.

It was Bacon who realized the importance for James of cooperation with Parliament, and he gave James good advice:

Look on a Parliament as a certain necessity, but not only as a necessity; as also a unique and most precious means for uniting the Crown with the Nation, and proving to the world outside how Englishmen love and honour their King, and their King trusts his subjects. Deal with it frankly and nobly as becomes a King, not suspiciously like a huckster in a bargain. Do not be afraid of Parliament. Be skilful in calling it, but don't attempt to 'pack' it. Use all adroitness and knowledge of human nature, and necessary firmness and majesty, in managing it; keep unruly and mischievous people in their place; but do not be too anxious to meddle, 'let nature work'; and above all, though of course you want money from it, do not let that appear as the chief or real cause of calling it. Take the lead in legislation. Be ready with some interesting or imposing points of reform or policy, about which you ask your Parliament to take counsel with you. Take care to 'frame and have ready some commonwealth bills, that may add respect to the King's government, and acknowledgement of his care; not wooing bills to make the King and his graces cheap, but good matters to set the Parliament on work, that an empty stomach do not feed on humour'.

It was a great pity, but James, who had made of his Scottish Parliament a pliant tool, ignored the advice. 'I am surprised', he remarked of Parliament, 'that my ancestors should ever have permitted such an institution to come into existence. I am a stranger and found it here when I arrived, so that I am obliged to put up with what I cannot get rid of'. That much he could accept – he simply could not manage without it; for the Crown was extremely poor, as continuing inflation reduced the royal revenue; from the middle of the sixteenth century prices had continued to rise until the reign of Charles I, when it has been estimated that in the course of a century the price of commodities had risen by some 300 to 400 per cent. Elizabeth had died in debt to the tune of £400,000, even though she had sold Crown lands during the last five years of her reign to the value of £327,000. Trade was flourishing, but the King was getting nowhere near his fair share of the customs revenue, and in direct taxation his subjects were paying him far less than was reasonable, probably no more than 2/6d per head of the population.

Therefore, even if James had been as thrifty as Elizabeth had been he could never have avoided an annual deficit; as it was he increased his own annual expenditure by some 50 per cent in his first six years, frittering it away on jewels for himself and gifts for his blood-sucking favourites and an extravagant Court. The result was that James was forced to ask Parliament for grants of money, not just to cover extraordinary expenditure necessitated by any emergency, but actually to pay for the day-to-day expenses of government; and this played right into the hands of the House of Commons, who would certainly use it as a lever and insist that their grievances should be redressed before they would agree to grant supply; furthermore, it encouraged Parliament's first open attempt to gain some measure of control over administration as well as legislation.

As the Commons knew all about James's theories of the Divine Right of all Kings and the subordinate position of Parliament, and as James seemed to be completely oblivious to the temper and dynamic of the House of Commons, an immediate clash was inevitable. On 11 January, before his first Parliament met on 19 March 1604, James issued a proclamation from Hampton Court 'concerning the choice of knights and burgesses'. County members, he had decided, should 'be selected out of the principal knights or gentlemen of sufficient ability within that county wherein they are chosen: and, for the burgesses, that choice be made of men of sufficiency and discretion without any partial respects or factious combination'. Care should also be taken to elect men of religious integrity, not bankrupts or outlaws 'but men of known good behaviour and sufficient livelihood, and such as are not only taxed to the payment of subsidies and other like charges, but also have ordinarily paid and satisfied the same'.

An attempt was also made in this proclamation to reform the electoral system, as sheriffs were charged:

not to direct any precept for electing and returning of any burgesses to or for any ancient borough town within their counties, being so utterly ruined and decayed that there are not sufficient resiants [residents] to make such choice, and of whom lawful election may be made; also to charge all cities and boroughs, that none of them seal any blanks, referring or leaving to any others to insert the names of any citizens or burgesses to serve for any such city or borough, but that the inhabitants ... do make open and free election according to the law, and set down the names of the persons whom they choose before they seal the certificate.

Had the subsequent election been conducted as James had prescribed great changes would have been made in the system of representation; it would, for example, have disfranchised the Gattons and Sarums, and the patron of many other rotten borough would have found his position somewhat constrained. Unfortunately, James made no effort at all to see the matter through; precepts *were* sent to decayed boroughs, and blank indentures, where the patron simply filled in the representatives' names *were* still as common. One more instruction in the King's proclamation was that all election returns were to be made into the Court of Chancery.

James's first Parliament got off to a bad start. On the first day the Commons were not summoned to the Lords as they should have been to hear the King's Speech; a yeoman of the guard forcibly prevented some burgesses who had arrived from entering the Lords' House, and the Commons were only calmed down by the King, who repeated his speech to them three days later at the presentation of the Speaker.

The first clash came over a question of privilege, the issue being to decide who should deal with disputed elections – the Court of Chancery, as James had maintained, or a Standing

Committee on Privileges, which the Commons under Elizabeth had claimed the right to examine returns. The actual case concerned Sir Francis Goodwin, an outlaw, returned as Knight of the Shire for Buckinghamshire. His election was certainly contrary to James's proclamation, so the Clerk of the Crown, who had issued the writs, refused the return, issued new writs, and Sir John Fortescue was then returned. The Commons summoned both Goodwin and the Clerk to the bar of the House and declared Goodwin to have been duly returned. James reminded the Commons that they 'derived all matters of privilege from him', thus drifting from the legal issue, where he had a good case – that outlaws were barred by law from Parliament and that all returns should go into Chancery.

After several weeks the Commons accepted the King's suggestion that the matter be resolved by sending out a third election writ to elect a new member. This counts as a defeat for James, and he did not protest at the Commons' settlement of two other disputed elections at Shrewsbury and Cardigan, and the Commons' right was not again challenged.

Their freedom of election, freedom from arrest (prompted by the Case of Sir Thomas Shirley in this same Parliament), and freedom of speech in Parliament were strongly claimed by the Commons in the Form of Apology and Satisfaction, drawn up at the end of the session on 20 June 1604, in terms which were not, however, acceptable to the House as a whole. It is not known whether the Apology was actually presented to James, but he cannot have been unaware of its contents, because it was read aloud in the House, so reports of it must have reached him.

In the Apology the Commons complained that in this first Parliament of the reign 'the privileges of our House, and therein the liberties and stability of the whole kingdom, have been more universally and dangerously impugned than ever (as we suppose) since the beginnings of parliament'. They insisted 'that our privileges and liberties are our right and due inheritance ... that they cannot be withheld from us, denied or impaired' and 'our making of request in the entrance or parliament to enjoy our privilege is an act only of manners'.

James's speech proroguing Parliament on 7 July was bad-tempered and tactless, far different from the iron-hand-in-the-velvet-glove technique, which Elizabeth had employed, and it certainly needled the Commons because James obviously still denied that their privileges were theirs by right.

When Parliament reassembled for its fourth session on 9 February 1610, the Commons' freedom of speech was again tested, this time on the question of 'impositions'. In imposing duties on luxury goods, and goods which competed with English products, James was following clear precedent and sound seventeenth-century economic thinking, and his right had been maintained by the judges in Bate's Case in 1606; but, like them, James again had to spoil a good case by claiming that his right to levy impositions was based on the 'special power and prerogative . . . inherent in the person of princes'. When the Commons nonetheless began to debate the legality of these impositions, the King sent word via the Council from Newmarket that the House was 'not to dispute of the King's power and prerogative in imposing upon merchandise exported or imported', and he later repeated his prohibition in person before both Houses of Parliament.

Understandably, the Commons' Petition of 23 May 1610, is not so polite as their Apology of six years before, for now they ticked off the King for holding up their discussions by his infringement of 'the ancient and fundamental right of the liberty of Parliament, in point of exact discussing of all matters concerning them and their possessions, goods and rights whatsoever'. James's conciliatory answer, though it settled nothing, did allow the great debate on impositions to go on from 23 June to 3 July.

This debate is important, because it raises the question of sovereignty. To William Hakewill, a Cornish M.P., the issue was whether the King could 'by his prerogative royal, without assent of Parliament, at his own will and pleasure, lay a new charge or imposition upon merchandize', and he believed he could not; but James Whitelocke in the same debate delved more deeply, for he believed that 'where the sovereign power is . . . there is the right of imposition'. Whitelocke's theory is certainly not in step with Tudor practice (at the time it attracted very little attention,

perhaps for this very reason), nevertheless it does give us an indication of the constitutional course that was being set out:

The sovereign power is agreed to be in the King: but in the King is a
twofold power – the one in Parliament, as he is assisted with the consent of the whole State; the other out of Parliament, as he is sole and
singular, guided merely by his own will. And if of these two powers in
the King, one is greater than the other and can direct and control the
other, that is *suprema potestas*, the sovereign power, and the other is
subordinata. It will then be easily proved [Whitelocke concludes]
that the power of the King in Parliament is greater than his power
out of Parliament, and doth rule and control it.

A similar argument, and one more typical of the age, because
it avoided the sovereignty issue, was expressed in the same debate by Henry Hobart, later Lord Chief Justice of the Common
Pleas, who concluded: 'Let no man marvel that the King hath
in some cases absolute power, as in war and such like. But he
cannot make laws without assent of Parliament. This I know
by the constant acknowledgment of the common law and statutes
throughout all ages.'

James dissolved his first Parliament on 9 February 1611;
his second, the 'Addled Parliament', met on 5 April 1614, and
straightway the Commons were increased by a rumour that 'some
one great man had by letters procured sixty voices' and they
suspected Court control; the King denied that he ever 'directly
or indirectly did prompt or hinder any man in the free election'.
Proceedings were taken against the Chancellor of the Duchy of
Lancaster, an M.P., who was accused of being an 'undertaker',
because he had interfered in the election at Stockbridge, and his
sequestration, it was felt, would enhance the prestige of the Parliament – 'It will be a caution to great ones hereafter how to write;
an encouragement to freeholders to use their own right in elections; and a good precedent for future ages that this shall be
punished in any how great soever'.

The King's electioneering, however, had really misfired,
because it was attempted in such a half-hearted way. Many of
the new members 'were such as had never been of any former
Parliament, and many of them young men and not of any great

estate or qualities'. They proved to be no less intractable than their
predecessors had been, some of them indeed being 'more fit to
have been among roaring boys than in that assembly'.

This Parliament had been called because the King wanted
money. After the failure of the Great Contract in 1610, Cecil had
succeeded in reducing the King's debts to £300,000; but Cecil
died in 1612, and rather than call Parliament James, then under
the influence of Carr, tried all manner of financial expedients –
except the obvious one, careful spending – and his debts soared
up again, to £680,000 in 1613.

Given this opportunity the Commons had no intention of
granting supply until their grievances had been redressed, so,
ignoring the King's threats of a dissolution, they proceeded to
resume their discussion on impositions, demanding a conference
with the Lords (which was refused), and then defending themselves warmly against an intemperate attack upon them by
Dr Neile, the Bishop of Lincoln. On 7 June James dissolved
Parliament, which, in two months, had not passed a single bill.

Remembering the intransigence of this second Parliament,
before his third Parliament met on 30 January 1621, James
issued a proclamation urging electors to choose men who could be
relied upon for their sincerity in religion; leading county men,
not malcontents likely to stir up trouble, should be chosen as
Knights of the Shires, while burgesses should not be young and
inexperienced men 'that are not ripe and mature for so grave a
council', nor 'curious and wrangling lawyers, who may seek
reputation by stirring needless questions'. The State Papers for
1620, in fact, show clearly that the Crown was recommending
candidates to many boroughs (as in 1624 'few towns were left
unsolicited by him') and that the Duke of Buckingham, with
the help of Lord Keeper Williams, acted as the King's election
manager.

Yet again the temper of the new House of Commons was hardly
as James would have wished. It immediately launched a furious
attack on the monopolists, whose numbers had been increased
since 1612, in spite of parliamentary protests against the abuse of
patents in 1606, 1610 and 1614; in particular, the monopoly for the

manufacture of gold and silver thread, held by Buckingham's brothers, was regarded as responsible for the shortage of bullion, which was contributing to a developing economic crisis in 1620. By their impeachment of Sir Giles Mompesson and Sir Francis Mitchell, who were found to have been extortionate licensees of inns, Commons and Lords, joining against the Crown, were really getting at Buckingham himself, who was fast becoming 'the grievance of grievances'. James sacrificed Mompesson and Mitchell, cancelled all outstanding patents of monopoly and allowed the now rampant Commons to proceed to the impeachment of Lord Chancellor Bacon on the admitted charge of receiving bribes.

In the second session of this third Parliament the Commons turned their attention to foreign policy. James's policy towards the Thirty Years' War, which had broken out in 1618, did not please the Commons, who wanted England to be actively involved on the Protestant side, a cause represented by the Elector Palatine, who had married James's daughter, the much loved Elizabeth, the 'Queen of Hearts'. The fear of Catholic conquest was again uppermost, and James's projected marriage alliance between his son, Charles, and the Spanish Infanta, redoubled the Commons' concern.

They petitioned the King 'speedily and effectually to take your sword into your hand' to aid 'those of our religion in foreign parts', and to abandon the Spanish Match. James, in his reply, spoke not of policy but of the prerogative:

Mr Speaker [he wrote] We have heard . . . that our distance from the Houses of Parliament . . . hath emboldened some fiery and popular spirits of some of the House of Commons to argue and debate publicly of matters far above their reach and capacity, tending to our high dishonour and breach of prerogative royal. These are therefore to command you to make known in our name unto the House, that none therein shall presume henceforth to meddle with anything concerning our government or deep matters of state, and namely not to deal with our dearest son's match with the daughters of Spain.

A second petition received a similarly cavalier reply. The Commons had claimed that to prohibit their discussions of such matters was to deny them 'the ancient liberty of parliament for freedom of speech, jurisdiction and just censure of the House ... the same being our ancient and undoubted right and an inheritance received from our ancestors'; whereupon James returned to his original and inevitable theme, expressed years before in the *True Law of Free Monarchies*, in maintaining that the privileges of the Commons 'were derived from the grace and permission of our ancestors and us', but if the Commons behaved themselves and kept 'within the limits of [their] duty' then he would as gladly maintain their 'lawful liberties and privileges' as his predecessors had done. If the Commons could not accept this then he would need 'to retrench them of their privileges, that would pare his prerogative and flowers of the crown'.

The Commons' Protestation, drawn up then after a week-long storm of resentment at the King's consistent denial of the claims and competence of the House of Commons, seemed to be just a restatement of the case for freedom of speech already presented in their Apology of 1604; but now they specifically claimed the right to debate all 'the arduous and urgent affairs concerning the King, state and defense of the realm and of the church of England, and the maintenance and making of laws, and redress of mischiefs and grievances which daily happen within this realm'. James himself, presiding over a meeting of the Privy Council, formally tore the Protestation from the Journals of the House, then issued a public statement reviewing the work of the session and justifying his action in dissolving Parliament, which he did on 6 January 1622.

The last round of the struggle between James and Parliament was won by Parliament. By 19 February 1624, when the last Parliament of the reign assembled, the amorous adventure of the Prince of Wales in Spain had turned sour, and he and the family favourite, Buckingham, had forced James to reverse his *beati pacifici* policy, to call another Parliament, and, bitterest blow of all, in his speech at the opening of this Parliament actually to request the Commons' advice on foreign policy; they were being asked, in effect, to arbitrate in a matter on which the Privy Council and the Royal Family itself were deeply divided.

The Commons advised war against Spain, as they had done in

1621; reluctantly and sadly, after a Joint Address from both Houses had left him with no alternative, James agreed, thus abandoning a policy in which he must still have sincerely believed. Lord Treasurer Cranfield, Earl of Middlesex, who had offended Prince Charles and Buckingham by continuing to support the Spanish alliance after their own embarrassed disenchantment, was gladly impeached by the Commons.

At the last James showed more understanding, more common sense than the Commons, and far more than his son and his favourite. Impeachment, he realized, was a dangerous instrument, and he was sure that Buckingham, in using it to dispose of a personal rival, was making a rod with which he might well be scourged himself; while as for his son, James assured him 'You will live to have your belly full of impeachments'.

Accumulated legislation, passed but not enacted in the 'angry' period from 1610 to 1624 was, in this parliamentary session of 19 February to 29 May 1624, when King and Commons were on their friendliest terms, brought up again and enrolled.

We have seen how in the last years of Elizabeth's reign the Commons were growing more disputatious, more energetic, more ambitious; the gentry were hungry for parliamentary experience and the pressure from outside for private bills increased the pressure on the parliamentary timetable, so that more frequent Parliaments were required. To restrain this parliamentary pressure, Elizabeth had had to exercise strict discipline; James, however, faced with the same pressures had neither the influence nor the power to keep them in check, and this in spite of his excessively 'busy' approach to Parliament – speeches on policy and prerogative at the opening and often during the course of many of the sessions, lengthy letters to the Speaker, messages to Privy Councillors, and positive encouragement of deputations from the Commons to wait on him – and so the initiative passed to Parliament.

His policies, his extravagance, his favourites, his interminable sermonizing caused opposition to become especially vociferous about grievances, and a Committee of the Whole House for Grievances first met in 1610 (when the Opposition assault on the

Government really began), its function to collect and go through with a fine tooth-comb the abundance of their grievances.

Small committees were accepted procedure under the Tudors, but from 1606 use was made of Committees of the Whole House, a procedure developed when the Speaker had absented himself for a few days on purpose to embarrass the Commons; in his absence the Commons chose their own chairman and debated freely, members speaking more than once to a motion, and without the Speaker's interference. By 1621 there were four such committees, their chairmen chosen from the new leaders of the House of Commons, and nearly all important questions were referred to a Committee of the Whole House – 'The order of the Hows is first to debate the business and hammer it well, then to putt it to Committees who are our executioners'.

The Speaker's guidance of the House in the interests of the Crown was also challenged in James's reign ; in 1614 and 1621 measures were taken to stop the Speaker curtailing discussion and stampeding the House into precipitate decisions, and in the debate on monopolies in 1621 Speaker Richardson was three times rebuked for 'intricating and deferring' the question, and for trying to close a debate without leave of the House; after all, said one member, the Speaker is 'but a servant of the House, and not a master, nor a master's mate'.

Privy Councillors were still important, but their influence and leadership were markedly on the wane. In the first Parliaments of James's reign there were fewer government servants in the Commons, due mainly to the King's failure in the management of elections, and only two Privy Councillors, an extremely careless omission on James's part. Formerly so strong on the small Select Committees, the development of larger committees relegated the Councillors to a secondary position. They still introduced measures – requests for subsidies, for example – but they had a hard job putting over policies which were increasingly so unpopular and, as a result, they were often ignored and even hissed; even Cranfield's brilliance in the Lower House before he was elevated to the peerage and the House of Lords in 1621, did not always impress the members, and the attacks on the presence in the Commons of the Attorney-General, Francis Bacon, were an indication of a general anti-Privy Councillor feeling.

James, in fact, ceased to manage his Council, which was increased during his reign to fifty members; it fell into factions, leaving real power in the hands of men like Buckingham, who, at the end of the reign and until his death in 1628, was wielding authority 'upon no merit but that of his beauty and his prostitution'.

Salisbury had preferred to control the Commons from his seat in the Lords, using conferences between the two Houses, and employing Bacon (though with great personal misgivings) as government spokesman in the Lower House. By 1610, however, this system had collapsed, and with the death of Salisbury in 1612 James himself took on the job of controlling the Commons, with what success has already been seen.

By 1621, too, the House of Lords had joined the Commons in opposition; and this opposition was becoming more organized, more sensitive to public opinion, more aggressive, the aggression coming especially from the lawyers – men like Sir Edward Coke and Sir John Eliot – who, by the 1620s, were the most important of the parliamentary classes.

Charles I and Parliament, 1625–9

The greatest contrast between Charles I and his father is seen in their attitude towards Parliament. No less sincere in his belief in Divine Right and the sacred office of a King, Charles made no such garrulous or constant reference to it. When he addressed Parliament his style was brief and to the point and, although on occasion he might send a message by one of his servants in the House, he kept no watchful eye on its deliberations, made no attempt to explain his policies; all he needed of Parliament was that it should grant him money whenever he required it, and, for the rest, to mind its own business.

Such an approach, though different from his father's, was no less dangerous. His first Parliament, which assembled on 18 June 1625, carried on as before in demanding that redress of grievances should precede supply; opposed the war with Spain by land, and granted an inadequate sum (two subsidies) for Buckingham's unexplained war plans; the legality of impositions was again questioned, and tunnage and poundage, from the time of Edward IV granted to the King at the beginning of his reign for life, was voted for one year only, pending an enquiry by the Commons (the Lords would not take part) into the whole system of indirect taxation.

The second session, held at Oxford because of plague in London, was greatly incensed by the only recently disclosed terms of the French marriage alliance, Charles's reversal of his promise of 1624 on applying the penal laws, and by Buckingham's undertaking to supply Richelieu with English ships to reduce the Huguenots at La Rochelle.

The association of Arminianism with Popery and the King's own involvement with the Arminian movement aroused the Protestant fervour of the country gentlemen in the Commons, just as Buckingham's undercover schemes aroused their anger that the King should be misled by 'young and simple counsel'. If money was needed it would only be granted if the Commons had confidence in the King's ministers, and at this time they had no confidence at all.

That Parliament should presume to choose his ministers was intolerable to Charles, and on 12 August 1625 he brought it to an 'unseasonable, unskilful and precipitate dissolution'. Before another Parliament assembled Charles determined to remove the chief opposition speakers from the House of Commons 'by charging them with employments that might make them incapable of the Parliament, presuming thereby others would be deterred, and the whole ability of that House extracted with those persons'. In November 1625 Sir Edward Coke, Sir Thomas Wentworth, Sir Miles Fleetwood, Sir Francis Seymour, Sir Robert Philips, Sir Guy Palmes and Mr Edward Alford were 'pricked' as sheriffs, and a sheriff, as Wentworth said when he heard the news of his own appointment as High Sheriff of Yorkshire, 'according to the received rule of our forefathers is tied to his county, as a snail to his shell'.

In spite of this tactic, the second Parliament of the reign that met on 6 February 1626, was still on the warpath; Buckingham was the enemy, Sir John Eliot the leader, and impeachment the weapon. Charles flew in defence of his friend: 'I must let you know', he told Parliament, 'that I will not allow any of my servants to be questioned amongst you, much less such as are of eminent place, and near unto me'. In this, precedent was undoubtedly on the King's side, for Parliament had not the power to punish a minister of the Crown who was simply carrying out a policy which had his master's approval, and who could have no crime proved against him. Eliot and Sir Dudley Digges were sent to the Tower, Eliot for eight days, Digges for five, for seditious words used in Buckingham's impeachment, and the commons were warned that 'Parliaments are altogether in my power for their calling, sitting and dissolution; therefore as I find the fruits of them good or evil, they are to continue, or not to be'.

From the House of Lords the King could expect no help at all, because he had also attacked their privileges by imprisoning in the Tower one of Buckingham's opponents, the Earl of Arundel, and by excluding another, the Earl of Bristol, from his place in the Lords in 1626. To save Buckingham, on 15 June, Charles dissolved this 'great, warm and ruffling Parliament'.

For the time being Charles successfully levied forced loans, the decision of the judges of the King's Bench in the Five Knights' Case in 1627, being given in his favour; but this did not bring in enough to support Buckingham's blundering foreign policy, and another Parliament was, therefore, essential. Attempts were made to influence the elections, but they failed; the counties ignored the High Constables' directives 'to give their voices for such gentlemen as shall be agreed upon by the more part of the magistrates', and made their own choice, while in some towns, generally thought to be Court strongholds, the Crown was even less successful than usual. Unfortunately for Charles, the Parliament called for 17 March 1628 contained the same strong opposition mixture as before, including twenty-seven members – Wentworth among them – who had just been released from prison for their refusal to pay the forced loan.

Arbitrary taxation and arbitrary imprisonment were, there-fore, immediate grievances of the House of Commons, and in the Petition of Right, which resulted from a conference between the Commons and the Lords, it was provided 'that no man here-after be compelled to make or yield any gift, loan, benevolence, tax or such like charge without common consent by Act of Parliament', and 'that no freeman . . . be imprisoned or detained' unless a clear charge be made. Although Charles was convinced that the Petition would 'dissolve the foundation and frame of our monarchy', he had no alternative but to accept; the Lords on this occasion stood firmly with the Commons against him.

Parliament's intention, as it had been in 1610, was not to dis-pute the King's legitimate prerogative, only to check his unlaw-ful abuse of power 'and to restore the ancient legal constitution to its proper balance'; but in doing this the problem of sovereignty was again aroused. To ensure the inviolability of the royal pre-rogative a section of the Lords had proposed the inclusion of this clause: 'We humbly present this Petition to Your Majesty not only with a care of preserving our own liberties but with due regard to leave entire that Sovereign Power wherewith your Majesty is trusted for the protection, safety and happiness of the people'. The immediately unfavourable reaction of the Commons shows just how uncertain were men's ideas of what sovereignty really meant. One, Alford, referred to Bodin, who 'saith that it is free from any condition; by this we shall acknow-ledge a regal as well as a legal power'. But John Pym was un-certain; 'I am not able to speak to this question: I know not what it is', he confessed. 'All our petition is for the laws of England, and this power seems to be another distinct from the power of the law. I know how to add sovereign to his person, but not to his power'. Indeed, if 'sovereign power' were the same as 'absolute power', perhaps even more, then if such sovereignty were con-ceded to the King, not even the law could limit his prerogative.

Acceptance of this clause would, in Coke's words, have over-thrown the Petition of Right. 'I know', he declared, 'that Pre-rogative is part of the law, but sovereign power is no parliamentary word. In my opinion it weakens Magna Charta and all our statutes; for they are absolute, without any saving of sovereign power ... Take we heed what ye yield unto, Magna Charta is such a Fellow, that he will have no sovereign. I wonder this sovereign was not in Magna Charta or in the confirmations of it. If we grant this, by implication we give a sovereign power above all these laws ... What it means here, God only knows: it is repugnant to our Petition: ... this is a Petition of Right, grounded on Acts of Parliament ...' The clause was unacceptable to the House of Commons and, on 7 June 1628, the Petition of Right received the royal assent.

At this point the Commons seemed to lose all sense of proportion and responsibility, and wilder men took control to turn the House into a hotbed of revolution; Coke, Wentworth and Digges gave place to the men who really gave Parliament its programme – Pym and Eliot. John Pym led Protestant opinion in another attack on the Arminian divines, Manwaring and Montagu; Eliot, with his great flair for denunciation, continued his assault on Buckingham, 'the cause of all our miseries ... the grievance of grievances'.

Charles replied to the Commons' remonstrance by proroguing Parliament to save his minister, realizing full well, as one unknown contemporary put it, that if Buckingham 'be decourted it will be the corner-stone upon which the demolishing of his monarchy will be builded: for if they prevail with this, they have hatched a thousand other demands to pull the feathers of royalty. They will appoint him councillors, servants, alliances, limits of expenses, and account of his revenues.' The Commons, in fact, were aiming to do just that, for the Petition of Right had laid down certain fundamental principles of government by which sovereignty must, inevitably, pass from the King and his Courts to an all-powerful Parliament.

Charles's third Parliament reassembled for what was to be its final session on 20 January 1629, and it was 'in an irritable humour'. The dispute with the King in the first session over tunnage and poundage had caused the Commons to table a disastrous remonstrance. 'That the receiving of tunnage and poundage, and other impositions not granted by parliament, is a breach of the fundamental liberties of this kingdom, and contrary to your Majesty's royal answer to the . . . Petition of Right; and therefore they do most humbly beseech your majesty to forbear any further receiving of the same, and not to take it in ill part from those . . . who shall refuse to make payment of any such charges.'

It was a very moot point whether tunnage and poundage had been included in the Petition of Right; but in any case there was certainly no justification at all for the Commons' virtual incitement of the people to refuse to pay the tax. This remonstrance clumsily destroyed the Commons' alliance with the House of Lords, which had been formed in 1621; and much public support was thrown away when the Commons frenetically took up the cause of a group of merchants, led by John Rolles, who had taken their advice and had refused to pay tunnage and poundage.

With Buckingham dead, peers who had been driven by his manner and methods into the ranks of the parliamentary opposition, now threw their weight on the side of the King. At this point a common-sense compromise on tunnage and poundage could easily have been made, but then common sense was not one of Sir John Eliot's many attributes, and the session ended in uproar as Eliot's Three Resolutions against Arminianism and those who collected or paid tunnage and poundage were put and carried, while Black Rod was hammering at the door of the Commons' Chamber and Speaker Finch was being forcibly held down in his chair.

The startling events of the year 1629 make it a real turning point in English history; for it marks the end of the epoch of Parliamentary monarchy, which had lasted – albeit fitfully – at least since the reign of Edward IV. With growing opposition in the House of Commons, disputes with the Crown had become ever more frequent but, although the exchanges had been sharp, and at times acrimonious, constitutional forms had nevertheless been observed. Now the actual physical restraint of the Speaker, who, though an officer of the House of Commons, was 'not the less the King's servant', and the blatant refusal to accept the

King's message of adjournment, indicated a fiercer, because a more revolutionary temper and the possibility of an eventual appeal to arms. The Three Resolutions of 1629 'were yet another attempt to impose the will of the Commons, as distinct from Parliament, on the nation', (J. P. Kenyon, *The Stuart Constitution*, Cambridge University Press, 1966); they represent the triumph, after 1628, of fanaticism over moderation. It was this same spirit, kept very much alive during the period of Personal Rule by the regular meetings of the leaders of the parliamentary classes, that re-emerged, fully armed with its clear political programme, in 1640.

Further Reading

MEYRICK H. CARRÉ, 'Francis Bacon, "The Peremptory Royalist" ', *History Today*, Vol. IX, No. 6 (June 1959).

G. P. GOOCH, *Political Thought in England from Bacon to Halifax*. Oxford University Press, 'Home University Library' (London, 1937).

W. H. GREENLEAF, 'The Divine Right of Kings', *History Today*, Vol. XIV, No. 9 (September 1964).

EVAN JOHN, *Charles I*. Arthur Barker (London, 1933).

M. A. JUDSON, *The Crisis of the Constitution, 1603–1645*. Rutgers University Press (New Brunswick, N.J., 1949).

MAURICE LEE JR, 'James VI, King of Scots', *History Today*, Vol. VI, No. 3 (March 1956).

H. R. TREVOR-ROPER, 'King James and his Bishops', *History Today*, Vol. V, No. 9 (September 1955).

H. R. TREVOR-ROPER, 'The Social Origins of the Great Rebellion', *History Today*, Vol. V, No. 6 (June 1955).

C. V. WEDGWOOD, 'The Causes of the English Civil War, A New Analysis', *History Today*, Vol. V, No. 10 (October 1955).

HUGH ROSS WILLIAMSON, *King James I*. Duckworth, 'Great Lives' Series (London, 1935).

D. H. WILLSON, *King James VI and I*. Jonathan Cape (London, 1956).
(See also pp. 178–9.)

C. H. WILLIAMS, *The Making of the Tudor Despotism*. Nelson, rev. ed. (London, 1935).

J. A. WILLIAMSON, *The Tudor Age*. Longmans, 2nd ed. (London, 1957).

G. W. O. WOODWARD, *Reform and Resurgence, 1485–1603*. Blandford Press, 'Blandford History of England' (London, 1963).

Interpretations of the Tudor Period

A Revolution in Tudor History?

PENRY WILLIAMS, 'Dr Elton's Interpretation of the Age', *Past and Present*, No. 25 (July 1963).

PENRY WILLIAMS, 'The Tudor State', *Past and Present*, No. 25 (July 1963).

G. R. ELTON, 'The Tudor Revolution: A Reply', *Past and Present*, No. 29 (December 1964).

W. T. MACCAFFREY, 'England: The Crown and the New Aristocracy, 1540–1600', *Past and Present*, No. 30 (April 1965).

D. C. COLEMAN, 'The "Gentry" Controversy and the Aristocracy in Crisis, 1558–1641', *History*, Vol. LI, No. 172 (June 1966).

The Tudors and Stuarts

KEITH FEILING, *England under the Tudors and Stuarts*. Oxford University Press, 'Home University Library' (London, 1927).

ROGER LOCKYER, *Tudor and Stuart Britain, 1471–1714*. Longmans (London, 1964).

The Stuarts

MAURICE ASHLEY, *England in the Seventeenth Century*. Penguin, 'Pelican History of England', 2nd ed. (Harmondsworth, 1960).

G. E. AYLMER, *The Struggle for the Constitution 1603–1689*. Blandford Press, 'Blandford History of England' (London, 1963).

GODFREY DAVIES, *The Early Stuarts 1603–1660*. Oxford University Press, 'Oxford History of England', 2nd ed. (London, 1959).

I. DEANE JONES, *The English Revolution: An Introduction to English History, 1603–1714*. Heinemann (London, 1931).

D. L. FARMER, *Britain and the Stuarts*. Bell (London, 1965).

CHRISTOPHER HILL, *The Century of Revolution, 1603–1714*. Nelson (London, 1961).

CHRISTOPHER HILL, *The English Revolution, 1640. An Essay*. Lawrence & Wishart, 3rd ed. (London, 1955).

Further Reading: General

The Reformation

DERYCK ABEL, 'The Elizabethan Archbishops', *History* Vol. VI, No. 10 (October 1956).

V. J. K. BROOK, *Whitgift and the English Church*. English Unive Press, 'Teach Yourself History' Series (London, 1957).

OWEN CHADWICK, *The Reformation*. 'The Pelican History o Church', Vol. 3, Penguin (Harmondsworth, 1964).

GORDON CROSSE, *A Short History of the English Reformation*. A Mowbray (London, 1950).

POWEL MILLS DAWLEY, *John Whitgift and the Reformation*. A. & Black (London, 1955).

A. G. DICKENS, *The English Reformation*. Batsford (London 1964).

PHILLIP HUGHES, *A Popular History of the Reformation*. Hollis Carter (London, 1957).

T. M. PARKER, *The English Reformation to 1558*. Oxford Universit Press, 'Home University Library' (London, 1950).

F. M. POWICKE, *The Reformation in England*. Oxford University Press (London, 1941).

H. A. L. RICE, 'Thomas Cranmer, 1489–1556, Archbishop of Canterbury', *History Today*, Vol. VI, No. 7 (July 1956).

HUGH ROSS WILLIAMSON, *The Beginning of the English Reformation*. Sheed & Ward, 'Canterbury Books' (London, 1957).

The Tudors

S. T. BINDOFF, *Tudor England*. Penguin, 'Pelican History of England' (Harmondsworth, 1950).

G. R. ELTON, *England under the Tudors*. Methuen (London, 1955).

H. A. L. FISHER, *Political History of England, 1485–1547*. Longmans (London, 1906).

J. D. MACKIE, *The Earlier Tudors, 1485–1558*. Oxford University Press, 'Oxford History of England' (London, 1952).

CHRISTOPHER MORRIS, *The Tudors*. Batsford (London, 1955).

A. F. POLLARD, *Political History of England, 1547–1603*. Longmans (London, 1913).

CONYERS READ, *The Tudors: Personalities and Politics in Sixteenth-Century England*. Oxford University Press (London, 1936).

C. R. N. ROUTH, *Who's Who in History*. Vol. II, England, 1485–1603. Basil Blackwell (Oxford, 1964).

C. P. HILL, *Who's Who in History*. Vol. III, 1603–1714. Basil Blackwell (Oxford, 1966).

J. P. KENYON, *The Stuarts*. Batsford (London, 1958).

J. A. R. MARRIOTT, *The Crisis of English Liberty*. Oxford University Press (London, 1930).

J. R. TANNER, *English Constitutional Conflicts of the Seventeenth Century*. Cambridge University Press (Cambridge, 1928).

G. M. TREVELYAN, *England under the Stuarts*. Methuen (London, 1904).

Principal Events, 1603–29

1603. March. James VI of Scotland succeeds as James I of
England
The Millenary Petition
Watson's Plot: Sir Walter Raleigh implicated, tried,
condemned to death, reprieved and imprisoned in the Tower

1604. January. The Hampton Court Conference
March–February 1611: James's First Parliament. Case of
Sir Thomas Shirley. The Buckinghamshire Election question
June. The Apology of the House of Commons
Peace made with Spain

1605. February. James enforces penal laws against Catholics
November. Gunpowder Plot

1606. Attempted legal union of England and Scotland
Bate's Case
Sir Edward Coke appointed Chief Justice of Court of Common
Pleas

1607. Establishment of Virginia

1608. Calvin's Case (*Post-nati*)
Robert Cecil, Earl of Salisbury, appointed Lord Treasurer
in succession to Earl of Dorset
Introduction of a new Book of Rates

1610. The Great Contract

1611. The Authorized Version of the Bible

1612. Death of Prince Henry, James's elder son
Death of Earl of Salisbury. Earl of Suffolk becomes Lord
Treasurer

1613. Sir Edward Coke appointed Chief Justice of the King's Bench
and Privy Councillor
Robert Carr becomes Earl of Somerset and Secretary of
State
James's daughter, Elizabeth, marries Frederick, Elector
Palatine

1614. *April–June: James's Second Parliament (The 'Addled'
Parliament)*
Death of James's Queen, Anne of Denmark

1615. Peacham's Case

1616. Case of *Commendams*
Coke dismissed from Privy Council and as Lord Chief Justice (replaced by Francis Bacon)
Publication of *The Workes of the Most High and Mighty Prince, James*
Death of Shakespeare

1617. Raleigh's disastrous expedition to 'El Dorado'
George Villiers becomes Earl of Buckingham (Duke in 1623)

1618. Outbreak of the Thirty Years' War
October. Execution of Sir Walter Raleigh on the 1603 charge
Earl of Suffok dismissed as Lord Treasurer. Treasury run by a commission

1620. James's son-in-law, Frederick, chased from Bohemia and the Palatinate
September. The 'Mayflower' sails

1621. *January–January 1622: James's Third Parliament*
February. Impeachment of Sir Francis Mitchell and Sir Giles Mompesson
March. Impeachment of Lord Chancellor Bacon
Lionel Cranfield becomes Lord Treasurer

1622. Lionel Cranfield created Earl of Middlesex

1623. February. Prince Charles and Buckingham set out for Spain
October. They return to England. Spanish Match ruined

1624. *February–March 1625: James's Fourth Parliament*
April. Impeachment of Lord Treasurer, Earl of Middlesex
The Monopolies Act

1625. March. Death of James I, accession of Charles I. Failure of Mansfield's expedition to regain the Palatinate
May. Marriage of Charles to Henrietta Maria of France
June–August: Charles's First Parliament
October. Failure of the Cadiz expedition

1626. *February–June: Charles's Second Parliament*
June. Impeachment of Buckingham, instituted by Sir John Eliot
September. Forced Loan. Chief Justice Sir Randolph Crew dismissed. Eliot, John Hampden and Sir Thomas Wentworth imprisoned

1627. France and England at war
      Failure of the La Rochelle expedition
      November. The Five Knights Case (Darnel's Case)
1628. *March–March 1629: Charles's Third Parliament*
      June. The Petition of Right
      August. Buckingham assassinated
      December. Sir Thomas Wentworth appointed Lord
      President of the Council of the North
1629. March. The Three Resolutions. Attack on the Speaker.
      Parliament dissolved
      Imprisonment of Eliot (until 1632), Benjamin Valentine
      (until 1640). Holles escapes abroad

Index